The
Dinner

The Political Conversation Your Mother Told You Never to Have

Terry Paulson, PhD

★   ★   ★

With Foreword by Martha House
President of the California Federation of Republican Women

The Dinner: The Political Conversation Your Mother Told You Never to Have

Copyright © 2004 by Terry Paulson

ISBN, print ed. 1-878077-11-2
ISBN, PDF ed. 1-878077-12-0
ISBN, LIT ed. 1-878077-13-9

First Printing 2004
Printed in the United States of America

Library of Congress Control Number: 2004092946
Paulson, Terry
The dinner: the political conversation your mother told you never to have/Terry Paulson.
ISBN 1-878077-11-2
First ed.
Includes a self-test

Amber Eagle Press
Post Office Box 365
Agoura Hills, CA 91376-0365
www.unitedwecanwin.com
info@unitedwecanwin.com

Book and Cover Design by Casa Graphics Inc.
Burbank, California
Printed by Central Plains Book Manufacturing
Winfield, Kansas

Acknowledgments...

To cite and thank all of the people who helped shape the comments and opinions expressed by the characters in this book would require more space than is available. You can find the primary sources for each chapter of *The Dinner* listed in the back of this book. The content in this book has been shaped by years of reading books and articles, listening to talk radio, watching political pundits discuss issues on television and following years of political campaigns. That same content has fueled many a dinner conversation of my own with Republicans and Democrats alike.

A special thanks goes to my parents, Ann and Homer Paulson, whose strong Republican values and patriotism helped shape my own views. The same goes for my loving wife, Lorie, who has shared my passion for the party and the principles our party represents. Our dinner conversations are often enlightening and always enjoyable!

I sincerely thank Dan Poynter of Para Publishing for his encouragement and publishing acumen, Ernie and Patty Weckbaugh of Casa Graphics for the cover and interior design and shepherding this book to completion, and Central Plains Book Manufacturing, my printing partner.

I want to thank all the Republican candidates who have had the *fire in the belly* needed to run for office. Win or lose, they cared enough to serve us all. And finally, I want to acknowledge the Federation of Republican Women, the largest all-women political organization in the world. It is their unsung grassroots activism that helped put most of our candidates in office.

What People Are Saying About *The Dinner*...

"Finally, Dr. Paulson has written a book that gets Republican principles and issues across in a way that people can understand and enjoy. After reading this book, many independents will wake up and realize that they were Republicans and they didn't even know it!" *–Martha House, President of the California Federation of Republican Women*

"Ronald Reagan was the master of communicating the ideals that mattered to most Americans, Republican and Democrat alike. *The Dinner* creates the warmth, reality and challenging ideas that Americans of all persuasions will again recognize as their dinner table conversations are given life. There's value here for everyone." *–Bob McCafferty, Manager, Governor's Office of Broadcast Services, Gov. Ronald Reagan*

"*The American Dream* is built on principles and driven by passion. *The Dinner* lets readers rekindle their passion for the principles that make this country great. Don't miss this thought-provoking book." *–Mark Isler, host of the Cable TV show, "Saving the American Dream"*

"Sometimes, we in the media get stuck settling for sound bytes. It's nice to be drawn into an informative and engaging dinner conversation about politics that you wish you could join. This book is a quick, must read before the November election for any thoughtful voter." *–Jane Wells, CNBC*

"Nothing is more compelling in politics than dramatic dialogue about powerful principles. *The Dinner* will move you – intellectually and emotionally – because it cares enough about America to risk addressing the issues that really matter. Please – for yourself and our country – read this book!" *–Scott McKain, author of "ALL Business is Show Business" and political commentator seen on FOX News Channel*

"*The Dinner* is both thought-provoking and entertaining at the same time. A great read and creative book! I really identified with all of Lee's positions, but I'm afraid this might make me a Republican rather than the moderate Independent I think I am! Do an encore on some of the other tough issues!" *–Dr. Tony Alessandra, author of "The Platinum Rule and Charisma"*

"The less you discuss something the less prepared you are to articulate your views. *The Dinner* shows you how people can disagree strongly yet avoid relationship tension. If you ever wanted to sell someone on a better way of looking at things, this book can be your model. Political discussions can become really rich interactions when you approach them in this way." *–Jim Cathcart, Author of "Relationship Selling," Lake Sherwood, CA*

Table of Contents

Foreword

"The greatest danger in any argument is that real issues are often clouded by superficial ones, the momentary passions may obscure permanent realities." –Mary Ellen Chase

As a community college board member I was invited to attend a leadership development program provided for the college administrators. As I listened to the speaker, I was impressed with his values, his message and his common-sense leadership insights. I approached him at the end of the program and inquired, "You're a Republican aren't you?" His radiant smile and affirming nod confirmed what I already knew in my heart—Dr. Terry Paulson was one of us!

After that day, there have been numerous times that I have arranged to have Dr. Paulson speak to our Federation of Republican Women audiences throughout California. His engaging sense of humor and professional speaking skills help him communicate Republican principles in ways that people can understand and appreciate. He not only informs; he continues to energize and inspire our members.

His own survey of California Republicans isolated six key principles that unite us: 1) Stand for smaller government & less government intervention/regulations; 2) Be a force to lower taxes; 3) Promote national and homeland security; 4) Help sustain the *American Dream* based on personal freedom and responsibility; 5) Promote educational excellence to leave no child behind; and 6) Foster a sound, free-enterprise economy. As Republicans, we are often our own worst enemies when we squabble over what divides us. Dr. Paulson reminds us that differences can be kept in perspective when we use our common passion to make a difference where we agree.

Over the last year, Dr. Paulson has used his serial, *The Dinner*, as a tool to bring Republican principles to life. Democratic policies are easier to convey in short sound bytes. Republicans need time to communicate their positions on the issues that matter most. There is no more important election than the one facing us this November. Our people need persuasive tools to communicate our positions to the Independents and Democrats who are unsure of their vote. His dialogues in *The Dinner* have provided our members with the words, facts and images that they need to fuel their own dinner conversations throughout the country.

As the current President of the California Federation of Republican Women (CFRW), I challenge you to read this powerful book. I also challenge you to bring your passion for the principles presented to a Republican group where you live. Our association has a unique mixture of older and younger women who together, provide a winning combination of experience and innovation. Our vast membership numbers, national network and strong finances allow us to make a difference for the Republican Party. Our strength comes from diversity of opinion, culture and experience. I want to thank Terry for letting me share my passion for *The Dinner* and the Republican Party it supports. Read it; reread it; share it with others; and then get involved and vote! That is both your privilege and your responsibility. Join the men and women of our party to leave footprints of patriotism that will make a difference for generations to come.

Martha House
President of the California Federation for Republican Women

Introduction

*"I have always believed that a lot of the
troubles in the world would disappear
if we were talking to each other instead of
about each other."* –Ronald Reagan

This book captures an informative and passion-filled dinner conversation between two couples a week before the presidential election November 2004.

The timely discussion takes place between two Democrats, a successful African-American talent manager and his wife, and a white professional Republican couple. Democrats, John and Lynn, own a talent agency in Hollywood representing a number of successful entertainers; Lynn has also actively supported Democratic candidates. Republican Lee is a professional speaker and consultant. His wife Kelly works in his office and is actively involved in the California Federation of Republican Women. The men had met at a professional conference where both were presenting; they had enjoyed a brief conversation and promised to get together on their return to LA. This is their first dinner engagement together as couples.

From the opening toast to the shared bill, both couples explore a political conversation few believe they can have. There is no name calling, just two couples trying to address issues impacting the important choice every American voter makes—whom will I vote for to guide and preserve this great country? This book allows you to listen in on an extended dialogue few experience in a lifetime. You will listen in as they explore the reasons they vote the way they do. It will help you contrast the parties as you make your choice. There is no obvious victory at the end of the book—only a sense that issues have been discussed freely and in depth…and, hopefully, with a sense of humor and warmth.

     Although there are many who have contributed to the information I share, I take responsibility for weaving pertinent information and important facts into conversations people might actually have if they took the risk to talk.

     At the end of the book, take the test provided to help you sort out what *you believe* on the values that separate Republicans and Democrats in America today. You may be surprised at how you score.

     Now, I hope you enjoy taking your own seat at *The Dinner...*

Chapter One

Talking About What Matters!

U SUALLY, FIRST DINNER CONVERSATIONS never touch on politics. Mothers don't suggest that their children *ever* talk about God or politics. This one night, Lee, Kelly, John and Lynn didn't listen to their mothers....

"To new friends," Lee made a toast, clicks all around. "I'm glad we could finally get together. Getting all four of *our* calendars coordinated is the greatest miracle of all! We meet halfway across the country, but it takes us four months to find a Saturday evening in LA for a *spontaneous* dinner between two couples. Now, let me start by saying how much I enjoyed sharing that panel with you in New Orleans."

"The honor is mine," John replied with a ready smile dipping his glass to Lee in a second, silent toast. "I must confess that my part was minimal. In fact, after hearing you speak at the conference, it was just glad to get more time to talk to you."

"Your comments were right on target," Lee countered. "But enough industry talk! Our wives know the truth about us, so we don't need to impress either one of them. And beside, you don't want to get a speaker like me talking, or you may not be able to shut me up!"

"You're lucky he didn't bring his *PowerPoint* slides," Kelly interjected. "That's when the dinners really drag!"

The laughter was interrupted as Lee looked up to see the waiter pass the menus around the table.

"Kelly, what do you do?" Lynn asked, being the first to look up from her menu.

"Now, I work with Lee in the office," Kelly replied. "I handle the company's accounting. But, to be honest, I spend much of my time in church work, and lately I've been very active with my local California Federation of Republican Women group. In fact, I talked Lee into walking our precinct with me earlier today. With the election next Tuesday, these last days are important in getting out the votes."

"You're *both* Republicans?" John asked, somewhat surprised.

"Be careful now," Lee said laughing. "Word has it that we Republicans are still an endangered species here in California. We are protected!"

"Seriously, you're a psychologist from LA…and *a Republican*?" John continued. "After listening to your comments at the conference, I wouldn't have guessed that."

"Ouch!" Lee said. "I always hope there is enough evidence in my comments that it shows. I know politics was not the topic that I was hired to present on, but, in spite of my efforts, it usually creeps into my comments at some point. But don't worry. I'm sure you're not alone. There are a lot of people who are sure that a psychologist from California couldn't possibly be a Republican."

"No, I'm just surprised," John replied.

"OK, we've confessed." Lee continued, "Now, by your reaction, and knowing that you are an African-American managing talent in the entertainment industry, does that mean that you might be a Democrat?"

"Only if I want to survive," John said laughing, cutting the early tension.

"There is a classic question in the speaking industry, 'Do you have to use humor as a professional speaker?'" Lee said. "I don't know who first said it, but the answer is always the same— 'Only if you want to get paid!'"

"In this case, no payment is necessary," John said with a slight laugh. "Lynn and I are both *willing* Democrats."

"I wouldn't expect anything less from you, or any American for that matter," Lee replied. "Voting in any election is too important to approach any other way. And don't worry. We have many friends who are Democrats, and we actually can still talk together without coming to blows."

"I like to vote the individual," Lynn added. "But most of the time that individual turns out to be a Democrat."

"I no longer vote individual." Lee responded. "I vote principles and *Rolodex*. I pick the party that supports the key values that are most important to me, and, unless the candidate is a criminal or unethical, I vote the party. There are no perfect candidates; they only exist in their own press releases and political ads. To me, it isn't just the person you elect; it's the *Rolodex* of contacts and resources that they bring to the office. They are the ones who help drive those values into action at the local, state or federal level."

> *"I do not wish to belong to the kind of a club that accepts people like me as a member."*
> –Groucho Marx

"You'd vote for a person you didn't respect?" Lynn questioned.

"I haven't had to. I'm sure all of us would agree that every party has some people it wishes would find another home, or at least get off the television talk shows so they can just vote quietly without further embarrassing their party. But no matter how obnoxious the person, both parties will *still* take their votes. I've decided long ago that you don't get to pick candidates a la carte! Now, you don't get to pick everybody in your family either, but they are still family."

"But think about some of the Republicans you have to put up with!" John countered.

"The Democrats have a few of their own that increase my blood pressure just by looking at them," Lee said interrupting. "Hey, I'll trade my *Queen of Hearts* for your *Jack of Clubs*. That's the trouble with politics today. You either paint hated pictures of the *enemy* or you settle for short one-liners that may grab the last minute votes, but you never get to hear constructive discussions of the issues that really count."

"I'm not overly impressed with either of the candidates we have this year!" Lynn added with disappointment.

"I'm *very impressed* with President Bush," Lee continued. "But I understand your comment. It's hard to be impressed with *any* candidate after the media and the political ads are done with them. The media and the opponents look for any mistake and broadcast it to the world. They ought to tell every candidate to send out their sin sheets early. If I ran, I'd say: 'Here's what you're going to find when you look, so you might as well know now. In fact, you might want to interview my mother! I'm sure she can add to my sin sheet.' I don't know about you, but I don't want perfect candidates. If you haven't made a few mistakes and can't admit them when you have, you won't be a very good leader."

"I like what one pundit said," John added. "If you want to discover your family history, just run for office."

"That's funny," Kelly said. "But sadly true."

"Are you ready to order?" the waiter said as he pulled up next to Kelly.

"Good idea. Saved by Greg the waiter!" Kelly responded. "I'm ready. I'll have the special salmon you described earlier. I'll have the salad with ranch on the side."

The orders were taken, the wine glasses filled, and the waiter left as quickly as he had appeared.

"I must confess that I think this is the closest I have been to a Republican I respect with time to talk," John interjected. "You said that you vote your values and core principles. What are the values and principles that matter most to you as a Republican?"

"Now you've done it!" Kelly said laughing. "Bring out the *PowerPoint* slides!"

"That's not nice, dear. Whose side are you on?" Lee countered with a smile, looking first at Kelly and then back at John and Lynn. "You've asked a fair question, and I'd be willing to answer it. Sometimes Kelly is concerned about my passion for my principles. I probably write an op-ed letter at least once a month to the local paper. I used to respond quickly with an e-mail message. Unfortunately, when you start a letter with 'Dear Democratic Bug Brains...,' You don't end up convincing very many Democrats to change their positions. I'm getting better at making my points with better clarity, but I will let you two be the judge of that. Of course, Kelly can certainly still kick me under the table if I get carried away."

"I'd like to know, too." Lynn joined in. "I have my own thoughts about what Republicans stand for."

"You may be surprised." Lee said with a smile. "I've found that many Democrats are really *Closet Republicans.* They stand for most of the principles that our party represents, but they just think God would strike them dead if they ever voted that way."

"My mother would strike me before God would be given a chance," John said with a smile. "Just don't tell me you're one of Bush's *compassionate conservatives!*"

"What a great place to start!" Lee said laughing. "You better take another sip of that wine. This is going to be an interesting dinner!"

Chapter Two

Caring and the Compassionate Conservative

"The worst thing you can do for those you love is the thing they could and should do for themselves." –Abraham Lincoln

★ ★ ★

"OK, Lee, tell us what it means to you to be a *compassionate conservative*," Lynn asked, taking a sip of wine.

"Wait a minute, before Lee gets started, let me share a simple explanation that I like to use," Kelly interrupted. "When it comes to defining what it is to care, being a *compassionate conservative* is no different from being a *compassionate parent*. We both have children, and I'm sure we both care about them deeply. We both can afford to give them pretty much anything they want, but we don't. Why? Because we care enough to discipline them, to set limits and to say 'No.' Learning to persevere and creatively overcome a few disappointments is the way they learn to appreciate the achievements they eventually earn. I think there is always a little bit of tough love in good parenting. And Republicans believe that there needs to be a little more tough love in Sacramento and in Washington."

"But even with tough love, there is at least a parent there to love!" Lynn asserted. "We are still there to give them a hug and pick up the pieces when they fall. There are a lot of people in America with no one to pick up the pieces. That's why government social programs are so important."

"I think that most Republicans would agree that there are some people who need a helping hand," Lee agreed. "America has always been a compassionate country where we help our neighbors, but the trick is finding a way to provide a safety net without making it a hammock that actually creates more problems than it helps."

"No one is asking for that," John replied.

"I'm not so sure about that, John," Lee said. "We have tried spending our way to being a very compassionate country. Lyndon Johnson's Great Society didn't work. We invested $5.4 trillion on welfare payments trying to win his *War on Poverty*. The investment would have been worth it, if it had worked, but it didn't work. The facts show that the poverty rate was falling before his *War* was launched. In 1950, the poverty rate was just over 30 percent. By 1966, the poverty rate had dropped to just below 15 percent without a *War on Poverty*. In 1992, after investing over $5 trillion to end poverty, the rate was still 14.5 percent. The poverty rate had dropped only two-tenths of one percent."

> *"I remember back when a liberal was someone who was generous with his own money." –Will Rogers*

"Even worse, the results of that type of compassion have been devastating," Kelly added. "Under the mantel of caring, we created programs that have helped undermine the will and character of millions of Americans by conditioning them to believe it is the responsibility of someone else to look after their needs."

"Republicans tend to measure compassion by how many

people no longer need government programs instead of by how many are served by them," Lee said. "We love our children, but eventually we want them to leave and be able to take care of themselves. We don't want them coming back at 30 and saying they want to move back in. Entitlements are not healthy in a family or in government."

"I don't know the numbers, but at over 14 percent living in poverty that still sounds like a lot of people who are poor," Lynn said with frustration. "What do you propose to do with those who remain in poverty?"

"Lynn, I'm going to try to say this as sensitively as I can," Lee said, pausing to find the right words. "You can never wipe out the poor. One reason is that the standard for being poor keeps rising. We have the wealthiest poor in the world. If you want to see poor, go to India, Africa, Cambodia, and even parts of Russia. Many people who are poor today in America will have things like televisions, cars, microwaves, even DVD players. Some of our citizens who qualify now as poor are people who are just temporarily between jobs. Economic realities as they are, people will not always have stable careers."

"The standard keeps rising because it costs more to live in America," John said in defense.

"That's right, and many of our poor keep expecting a higher standard of living. But they expect it to be at someone else's expense," Lee continued. "But this isn't just a money issue. The myth is that throwing more at poverty helps. There is no evidence that it does. Many Democrats keep referring to the Reagan years as the *Decade of Greed*. That was a decade of tremendous achievement and economic growth, not greed. True greed is when one group of Americans envies what others have worked to earn and somehow expect others to pay for their failure to achieve and, frankly, their irresponsible choices."

"That's cold," Lynn said. "That's certainly not very compassionate."

"No, I think that is true caring," Lee replied quickly. "I'm afraid that over the years, the Democrats have moved from being the party of the worker to the party of the non-worker. By continually expanding government programs that increase dependence, they have wasted capable, productive members of our country by making it almost noble to be poor."

"That's a pretty tough message, and not a very popular one!" John confessed.

"This message is no more popular to citizens who have come to expect free programs from the government than it is for teens to accept curfews," Lee continued. "It doesn't make you a popular parent to set limits, but it does make you a better parent. My son never said, 'Thank you dad for saying 'No' to me today. I know I was disappointed, but you helped make me more of a man. I'd like to come back tomorrow and have you disappoint me again!' If he said that, I would have sent him to therapy. As a parent, I'd rather be respected than liked. As a country, I would rather people earn self-respect than settle for dependence. To most Republicans self-reliance is not an outdated value. We believe it is a transforming value that has helped make us what we are as a country."

"This sounds so good in theory," John tried to counter.

"I think it is the Democrats who say that they are helping by passing more and more government programs that *sound good in theory*," Lee countered. "It sounds like caring, but it doesn't work. Life is difficult, and it's getting tougher. Winning at the game of life takes work, struggle, failure, experience, successes, new learning, more failures, creative thinking, and it always involves a challenging journey. Parents who protect their children or politicians who protect their citizens from the lessons learned from that struggle don't do them any good."

"What about the children who through no fault of their own are left with irresponsible parents who can't care for them?" Lynn asked.

"I remember a black physician I talked with at county hospital," Kelly interjected. "He told me about a young woman on welfare he overheard speaking to her daughter. The mother pointed to her case worker who had just entered the clinic and said, 'That's my case worker. Someday you will grow up and have your own case worker, too.'"

"No," Lynn sighed.

"The doctor wanted to shake her," Kelly said softly. "He held his tongue and shared his frustration with me."

"I think that is an extreme example." John replied.

"Even if it is an extreme example, that is one child who is being taught to expect nothing more than a welfare check and food stamps," Lee admitted. "Let's not forget the children Lynn talked about. Should we not care enough to make achievement pay off more than dependence and powerlessness? Out of wedlock births in America became a major problem when it paid more to have a child out of wedlock than it did to stay in school."

"It's hit our black youth the hardest," Lynn confessed.

"No matter what the race, those young women were hurt, not helped, by government programs," Kelly said. "When we were their age, we would have been ashamed. We would have depended on our families, not the government, and we would have probably given up our children to adoption. I think we should reintroduce a little more shame for people who have children out of wedlock and honor young people who have cared enough to give their children for adoption. I don't know about you, but I still think it's best that a child have both parents to start out with."

"Having children out of wedlock is not acceptable in our home." John said with resolve. "We've made that very clear. They also know that we expect them to go to college."

"I told you that you were more Republican than you thought." Lee said with a smile.

"Not yet, I'm not," Lynn said, reacting to the label. "I'm not so sure that *all the Republicans* are into caring for anybody. I think that they just don't want to pay the bill for those in need."

"I'm sure there are some people from both parties who would rather have someone else pay the bill," Lee agreed. "But I think depending on government programs allows people to say, 'I don't have to love my neighbor; the government loves my neighbor.' I think charity and giving are important for each of us to do personally. We need to take care of our neighbors in need. Like many, we take that seriously as a couple. But I don't believe in electing politicians who will take from the wallets of our most wealthy citizens to pay for *MY* charity. That's not right. If we all want to help, we should all have to pay part of the bill for the people in need."

"That's a good point, but, obviously, some programs are necessary," Lynn said. "How do you decide which programs to fund?"

"Unfortunately, once a government program is started, few are stopped," Lee confessed. "We need politicians in our state and federal government who will invest our limited federal, state and local budgets into programs and services that produce real results. And results mean—those programs which get people back into being productive members of society. We need to have politicians with the courage to cut programs that do not add value. That kind of courage is not easy to find. Not many in either party seem to have the courage to stand up to the name-calling they'll receive. You know the names—'mean-spirited, racist, sexist, poor-hating Republicans who want children to starve!'"

"The Statue of Liberty on the East Coast needs to be supplemented by a Statue of Responsibility on the West Coast." —Victor Frankl

"That was just what I was going to say," Lynn said with a smile. Everyone joined in the laughter.

"It's not a crime to be poor and to go through difficult times," Kelly said. "We have a moral obligation to help those who truly can't help themselves, but it is also wrong to take someone's money and give it away with no concern for whether it is wasted. Even more tragic, I think it's making the problem worse."

"In America, all citizens are guaranteed 'the pursuit of happiness,' not happiness dumped in their laps," Lee added. "But after listening to Kerry and Democratic leaders I am convinced that caring is supposed to mean that every American is entitled to happiness, healthcare, welfare, education, a high wage, and a secure retirement... whether they have earned it or not. For most Republicans, the push out of the hammock may be the most caring thing America can do to help everyone realize their own capabilities and their own responsibilities."

"The next thing you are going to tell me is that the *American Dream* is still alive and well for all Americans," John said with sarcasm.

"I didn't know that you had premonitions," Lee countered. "I couldn't have said it better. We've *both* lived that dream. I'd hate to think we are the last."

The waiter apologized for interrupting their dialogue.

"No problem," Lee said. "It's always the right time for good food."

Placing their salads on the table, the waiter turned first to Kelly, "Would you like pepper on your salad?"

"No thank you," Kelly replied.

"Certainly, I'd love some," Lee responded. "I might as well have my salad as spicy as our conversation!"

"I'll take some pepper, but just a couple twists." Lynn said. "Too much *spice* gives me nightmares... whether that's an *American Dream* or otherwise!"

"No nightmares. I promise," Lee countered with a smile. "Just pleasant dreams!"

Chapter Three

Saving the American Dream

"Some regard private enterprise as if it were a predatory tiger to be shot. Others look upon it as a cow that they can milk. Only a handful see it for what it really is— the strong horse that pulls the whole cart."
–Winston Churchill

★ ★ ★

"Why are you so sure America is still the land of opportunity?" John asked, taking another bite of his salad.

"It's not hard to prove that America is still the land of opportunity," Lee said with confidence. "America is still passing *the gate test*. Just look at the way the gate swings at the border. There aren't many people trying to *get out* of America!"

"And the people coming to America aren't just the poor, huddled masses," Kelly added. "Many have given up careers as physicians or university faculty to come to this country. Their credentials often mean little here. They come to start over because this is America, and they *still believe* that dreams are made here."

"A lot of those immigrants who came to California expecting to find their pot of gold are sniffing more golden poppies than actual gold," Lynn said with frustration. "With the budget troubles we've had over these last few years, the *California Dream* looks like it's on its last leg."

"It isn't just the immigrants who are hurting. When people and businesses are over-taxed and over-regulated, they migrate to greener pastures, or at least to states that let them keep a bit more of *their green*," Kelly added.

"No pity party, please! There is still opportunity out there," Lee added. "The economic turnaround is continuing. In fact, the economic growth in California is better than in many other states. I think Arnold, our very own *Governator,* has been doing a good job with the choices he has made since being in office. Look, California has had economic struggles before, and we've always found our way through them. I was speaking in Iowa. Over dinner, one man couldn't resist a jab at our plight. He said with pleasure, 'I'm *glad* the *California Dream* is dead! I'm so tired of hearing how wonderful California is!'"

"What did you say?" Lynn asked.

"Are you kidding? California is the only state that has ever had a dream. When was the last time anyone ever heard about the *Iowa Dream*?"

"Did he hit you with a corn stalk?" John said laughing.

"No, but I made sure that I said that *after* all the evaluations were collected!" Lee said smiling.

> *"Who among us would trade America's future for that of any other country in the world? And who could possibly have so little faith in our American people that they would trade our tomorrows for our yesterdays?" –Ronald Reagan*

"Unless you want to be left nibbling on a few of those

corn stalks, you better finish some of your salad greens before our waiter brings the entrée," Kelly interjected.

"OK, I'll finish my salad, but let me finish my story," Lee conceded. "The *California Dream* may struggle at times, but even when it struggles, it is building a new base of economic strength. The weather is too nice here for everyone to leave for greener pastures. We have 34 million people in this state. That's a lot of people who can buy the products and services that new companies create. Alone, California would be the 5th largest economy in the world. The bad times sow the seeds for even better times and an even broader economic recovery."

"I have a feeling you're going to explain how that happens!" Lynn said, now more interested.

"Welcome to capitalism in action," Lee added. "In the bad times, many good people lose jobs and can't find new ones. As a result, some very bright people are left with house payments they can't afford."

"This is *good* news for California?" John asked.

"It will be," Lee continued. "Capable people who can't find jobs have to find a way to pay the bills. They start their own businesses in their garages—businesses they were too comfortable to risk even dreaming about. Each of them finds a need and fills that need. Within four years of those economic downturns, the economic base of new small businesses is there to fuel a recovery and hire more people. We may not be all the way back yet in California, but we will be."

> *"For 150 years, America has consistently performed in the steady 3% GDP growth area. What is the secret? America has been successful because Americans believe that in this country you earn success. Whether it is entirely true is not important. People believe in the doctrine of equal opportunity and the American Dream."*
> *–Marvin Zonis*

27

"Why are you so sure that this is going to happen?" Lynn asked.

"This is America, and it has happened over and over again in our history," Lee said without hesitation. "We have innovative entrepreneurs, ready investment capital, good workers, and enough freedom and regulatory restraint to keep the dream alive! Now, if I forgot to tell you, the *American Dream* based on personal freedom and individual responsibility is a cornerstone principle of the Republican Party. You've both lived the dream. You've earned your success. You should be part of the party that is dedicated to keeping that dream alive for your children!"

"You aren't giving up are you?" Lynn said laughing.

"Republicans never give up!" Kelly chimed in. "We can't afford to give up in a state where the Democrats have us outnumbered."

"It's more than who wins elections," Lee countered. "Only a society that allows individuals to develop and use their unique talents will ever reap the benefits of human greatness. The greatest tragedy we face as Americans is the number of citizens who no longer believe that they either have those unique skills or any hope of benefiting from them. I'm afraid that many of our young people are losing that sense of optimism for the future and their place in it."

"What do you mean?" Lynn asked.

"I had a speaking colleague who did programs for teens on how to start their own companies. They promoted the programs in America and had a hard time getting our teens to attend," Lee confided. "My theory is that they don't feel a need to succeed for themselves. They live in our homes. They go on our vacations. And they don't have to work to earn either. It's too easy for our youth to take what they have for granted. Even worse, they seem to feel that they are entitled to all these blessings without having to earn them. That same speaker went to Singapore and sent out one brochure. Two thousand teens showed up with pens in hand ready to learn how to start their own company."

"That's frightening!" Lynn reacted.

"That's opportunity, and the rest of the world is taking it. Don't get me started," Lee continued. "Schools in the U.S. grant about 70,000 undergraduate degrees in electrical engineering a year. In contrast, China produces 200,000 electrical engineers and graduates over 600,000 engineers every year! Fifty-four percent of U.S. engineering doctorates are foreign students. Of the more than 400,000 Chinese who have studied overseas in the past two decades, over 140,000 have moved back to China. China is in the process of opening 35 special software universities this year alone. We think of China as a low-cost manufacturing country. They are taking our dream and driving it with a technological edge that will be tough to beat! And they aren't alone. The world has seen what we have, and they want it. Whether they immigrate here or they connect to us via the Internet, they are coming to compete. The good news is that the better they get, the more that they can afford to buy from us. A growing world economy is not a problem as long as we keep our own hopes and dreams alive for our children."

"We make our children earn their way," Lynn stressed.

"Your Republican values are showing," Lee chided Lynn.

"Good parents come on both sides of the political divide." John interjected.

"I'm sure that is true," Lee agreed. "Unfortunately, I'm afraid that not enough parents in America agree with us. Getting our youth to believe in the dream is tough business today. But now, I've got to dive into this salad before Kelly stuffs it in my mouth!"

"Not a bad idea." Kelly said laughing.

"But fear not!" Lee said waving his fork in the air. "I have a few more stories to tell."

"I'm sure you do, and we look forward to hearing them... *I think!*" Lynn smiled and slid her fork into her own salad.

Chapter Four

Getting Others to Believe in the Dream

"Keep away from people who try to belittle your ambitions. Small people always do that, but the really great make you feel that you, too, can become great." –Mark Twain

★　★　★

"Lynn, you said you stressed education and made your children earn their way. I couldn't agree more." Lee said with respect. "We did the same with Mike. Some children you can give things to, but Mike wasn't one of those kids. He never quite learned the importance of saving for the things he wanted until he wanted a car at sixteen."

"A car at 16?" John said laughing.

"Yes, according to Mike, *everybody* gets a car," Lee said. "I told him that I didn't think that was true, but that even if it were true, it would be everyone *minus* one."

"Good for you," Lynn added, joining in the laughter.

"He didn't stop with that. Mike said his birthday was coming up, and he asked if I could give him *anything* towards his car," Lee continued. "He's willing to settle for anything at that point. I used a great line that I stole from Bill Cosby, 'I'll match what your friends will give you.'"

"That's a good one. I'm writing that one down," John said pulling out his Palm Pilot.

"I told him that there were four ways to make money legally in America," Lee said, knowing that he was now in his element. "You can be an entrepreneur; find a need and start a company to fill that need. You can also create something somebody needs by being an author, an artist or an inventor. If you don't have what it takes to create or start your own company, you can try selling. Just build strong customer relationships and earn a commission selling them something they are willing to pay for. And finally, if none of those ring your chimes, you can find a way to use the gifts God has given you to earn a living."

"That about covers it." Lynn said, now enthused.

"I also told him one final hint worth learning," Lee added. "Too many people make a good living but spend every dime they make. No matter how much people make, they need to set aside a portion of that income to create wealth. My final observation may have been a bit tough; I told Mike that he had invested in the *wrong* CD's!"

"You are tough!" John laughed. "But you are right!"

"Mike was disappointed. But he wanted that car, and he ended up working hard for it. Now, his first car was not that great, but it was his. He worked all summer and saved *every* dime," Kelly said with pride. "We did help with the insurance. Lee isn't as tough as he sounds."

"What a wonderful story and an important lesson," Lynn replied, not yet convinced. "But you've seen the papers. There is a growing gap between the rich and the poor. Not everyone is *living* the *American Dream*."

"The gap should never be a problem as long as the poor are also doing better," Lee countered. "The success of the rich doesn't take money from the poor. The charity of the poor should be to wish the rich well. After all, it's the rich who invest their capital to create business opportunities that put the poor to work. Capital needs labor willing to work and save; labor needs applied capital willing to take a risk on new dreams. Both need a government that will insure that they will continue to be free to dream dreams and to reap the benefits of making those dreams come to life. It may not be perfect, but there is no other country that has had the results that we have had."

"But what about the 30 million poor in America we keep reading about?" Lynn continued.

"There are two things worth noting about America's poor," Kelly interjected. "Remember what I said earlier—our poor live to a higher standard than the world's poor. And secondly, most of *our* poor don't stay poor! Rich people live well everywhere in the world. But what makes America so special is that it provides a relatively high standard of living for the common man. It's a place where line workers stand in line to pay $4 for their favorite latte at Starbucks, where many maids drive cars, and where laborers often make enough to take their families on vacation to Europe."

"Kelly and I are partial to Folgers Instant coffee, but our son spends his hard-earned money on Latte almost every week. I mean, that's America," Lee chimed in. "In the 80's, there was a CBS television documentary that focused on the miseries of the poor in America. To embarrass Ronald Reagan, the Soviet Union showed the documentary to their citizens, but it backfired. Ordinary people in Russia saw that many of the *poorest* Americans had TV sets and cars while *their middle-class* had to stand in line for bread."

"I read about one young man from Bombay, who, when asked why he was so eager to come to America, replied, 'I really want to live in a country where the poor people are fat,'" Kelly added.

"OK, America's poor certainly are better off than the

33

world's poor, but they live in a world that reminds them every day how poor they are," John asserted. "Staying poor is still no *American Dream.*"

"Most American poor *don't* remain poor," Lee stayed his ground.

"How can you be so sure of that?" Lynn countered.

"That's a good question, Lynn, because our media doesn't like talking about American success stories." Lee answered. "There is always a base of Americans who are out of work and would for a period of time be classified as poor. There is a chronic poor that we see on our streets. But how many of those reported 30 million poor actually remain poor over time? The University of Michigan has reported on research that followed large samples of poor Americans for decades to assess their progress. I won't bore you with all the data, but I can summarize the results. Over several decades only 1 out of 20 `poor' Americans will stay poor, while 13 will become `middle class' and 6 will become `rich.' Yes, there is a small, chronic poor population, but over all, America raises all boats, if you are willing to row!"

"Why don't we see these reports?" John asked.

"I think victim thinking sells better!" Kelly replied.

"I know some people are very well meaning in their concern, and we should care about the truly poor," Lee said with passion. "But this country has not run out of opportunity. All it takes for the *American Dream* to work its magic is for more citizens to claim it for themselves. Do something better. Do it cheaper. Do it faster. Make choices. Fail, get up and make new

"I don't believe in a law to prevent a man from getting rich; it would do more harm than good. So while we do not propose any war on capital, we do wish to allow the humblest man an equal chance to get rich with everybody else." —Abraham Lincoln

choices, and succeed."

"You certainly are optimistic," Lynn said smiling.

"Optimism is infectious. If you don't look out, you may catch it!" Lee said matching her smile for smile. "The promise of America is freedom to succeed and fail, nothing more. It wasn't greed that made Ronald Reagan unbeatable in the 80's; it was his optimism and his belief in American citizens like you and me. The Republican legacy of optimism doesn't rest in Washington or in Sacramento. It rests in citizens working individually and together to invent a better future. Reagan appealed to our hopes and our confidence instead of our doubts and our fears. So, why am I still so optimistic? Why not? I am an American."

"OK," John replied. "I bet you think it helps that you are a *Republican* American."

"No," Lee answered quickly. "I trust *Democrats* benefit from that same dream. I know many who have. I'm looking at two, right now."

"We've been fortunate, but I'm not so sure that *every* race shares equally in that optimistic dream," Lynn said sadly. "Republicans are doing everything they can to put an end to affirmative action programs."

"I see Greg is bringing the entrée. Now, let's all promise not to throw any food!" Lee said, showing mock concern. "Seriously, I'm glad you brought that up. There are no two people I would rather talk about affirmative action with than you two."

"You are brave," John replied. "I can't even talk sanely with Lynn about that subject."

"I have found in my years of experience that husbands and wives often treat each other better in public," Lee said. "That bodes well for our mutual survival. Besides, this food looks way too good to throw."

"OK, Lee." Lynn smiled. "I promise no throwing, but you are talking about one of the reasons I *couldn't vote Republican*."

"I'm glad this is a long dinner," Lee said. "We may all need the time."

Chapter Five

Beyond Affirmative Action

"I have a dream that my four little children will one day live in a nation where they will not be judged by the color of their skin, but by the content of their character."
—Martin Luther King, Jr.

★ ★ ★

"So, you support an end to affirmative action?" Lynn said, taking the offensive. "And I suppose you think racial bias is a thing of the past!"

"John was right!" Lee answered, trying to bring lightness to his tone. "You are tough. Why don't you take a bite out of that delicious looking salmon instead of me!"

"No fangs," Lynn replied with a knowing laugh. "I promise."

"Of course, racism and bigotry still exist," Lee continued. "Both parties need to condemn racism, and violators need to be prosecuted and punished when anti-discrimination laws are broken. But we can't cure discrimination with *more* discrimination. I remember when Clinton used to say, 'Mend it; don't end it.' I prefer a more Republican slogan, 'Abolish it; don't polish it.'"

"Slogans don't hold much weight in the face of years of slavery and racism," John said, joining in.

"Slavery in America ended in the 19th Century, and over half-a-million Americans gave up their lives settling whether it would come to an end," Kelly interjected. "Unfortunately, I think racism is alive and well in all races. There are white racists,...black, brown, red and yellow racists."

"Not all races experienced slavery," Lynn interjected.

"Before a new war begins at this table, let's stay focused on affirmative action," Lee asserted. "Afirmative action was designed to affirm and support opportunity for black Americans, but because of legal intervention and interpretation, it has come to mean a commitment to preferences, set-asides or quotas. It wasn't designed that way, but it has become that. So, the point remains—new discrimination does not make up for past discrimination. If we have any affirmative action, it ought to result in support for *any* American who needs a leg up, not just for black Americans."

"I'm afraid that more black Americans *need* that leg up," John confessed.

"Maybe that is because affirmative action isn't working. In fact, it may be hurting." Lee shared with conviction. "I heard Ward Connerly say...."

"I don't want to even *hear* his name," Lynn interrupted. "Connerly is just another one of the right-wing conservatives' *black mascots!*"

"Wait a minute," Lee said with concern. "To give a black liberal that kind of label would get you hate headlines in the *LA Times*! I have heard Ward Connerly speak. He's too eloquent and informed to be anybody's mascot. I disagree with many white colleagues and friends who are more liberal than I, but I don't question their convictions for the positions they hold. I'm afraid that for a black American to have the courage to admit he or she is a conservative is an open invitation to 'hate' mail. Lynn, you certainly aren't suggesting that every black conservative is a traitor to their race, an *Uncle Tom*, or, as you call Ward, a conservative *black mascot*? What about Larry Elder, Walter Williams, Star Parker or Thomas Sowell? Or are we to believe that all blacks must think a certain way to be a *true* black?"

"Of course not!" Lynn confessed. "I just think Ward Connerly goes too far."

"I know that both sides can play the blame game," Lee said. "But the name-calling is far too predictable: 'It's your fault because you're a racist!' 'No, it's your fault because you expect something for nothing.' 'It's white skin privilege.' 'No, it's reverse racism!' And on and on it goes."

"Well, whites share more than their share of the blame." John replied.

"I'd be the first to admit that loudmouths of all races will always be with us and will keep saying obnoxious and foolish things," Lee agreed. "But it would be wonderful if more opinion leaders who engage in what passes for public discourse on this matter would recognize an obvious reality—It hardly matters who is responsible for things being screwed up! The only relevant question is, 'How do we make things better?'"

"In the next stage of the civil-rights struggle, the true heroes will be those who focus inward as well as outward, who don't just make demands on government but who demand discipline and responsibility from themselves and their children. Continuing to foster self-reliance and self-regard is just as important as combating racism in others."
—Steven Roberts

"Have you ever gone to the Simon Wiesenthal Center's Museum of Tolerance in West Los Angeles?" Kelly asked.

"No, is it worth seeing?"

"Yes, it is," Kelly replied. "I love the way they set the stage for those entering. When you arrive at the entrance, you are asked to make a choice by which door you wish to enter. One door, reads, 'If you have no prejudice, enter here.' The other reads, 'If you have prejudice, enter here.' If you try to enter the door indicating you have no prejudice, the door does not open. You are forced to use the other door. I think it's time we all stop pointing fingers, and start taking responsibility for our part of the problem."

"Kelly, I don't think the door operates that way anymore. Too many people got upset at being told they were prejudiced. So, in that spirit, let me get back to an unopened door—Ward Connerly's statement. After all, it isn't who makes a point; it's what's said that ought to count," Lee continued. "Ward says what many are afraid to say, 'Contrary to popular opinion, slavery has not been ended. It is alive and well in America. We call it *affirmative action.*' To Ward and many others, affirmative action has outlived its usefulness. Far too many black Americans remain enslaved to its premise that you can't succeed without it."

"Calling it slavery doesn't negate the reality of the need," John countered. "You may find this hard to believe, Lee, but some blacks can't just pull themselves up by their own bootstraps."

"When the court rulings ended affirmative action quotas in state-supported universities in California and Texas, the Democrats screamed that it would end black students' access to college," Kelly replied. "They said it would introduce the 'resegregation of higher education.' They failed to report that affirmative action wasn't working; students were failing because they were in over their heads. In reality, the end of affirmative action in California and Texas state institutions meant that fewer black students went to Berkeley or Austin, and far more went to other state colleges and universities in the same systems. More are succeeding now. Instead of being artificially forced to compete with students where the standards are higher and then failing, more students are succeeding where the standards are at a level that matches their academic capabilities. That's true caring."

"Many black Americans are getting ahead in school and in America," Lee said, "More would be getting ahead if we could cut off the black leaders and public-funded programs that depend upon keeping a large percentage of the minority populace in rage and in dependency."

"That sounds *very* Republican!" Lynn said, taking a stab at her salmon. "Blame the victims, and if that doesn't work, blame Jesse Jackson!"

"I used to respect Jesse Jackson, but I don't anymore." Kelly countered. "He used to stand for changing attitudes—he was into turning victims into victors."

"What do you mean?" Lynn asked.

"His Rainbow/PUSH Coalition was constructive, but, now, he seems to spend most of his time shaking down the government and corporate America for millions, and there are some real questions as to how those funds are used," Kelly stressed. "Instead of profiting on victim thinking, he ought to move his Rainbow Coalition to Africa to put an end to the slavery that is *still* thriving there today. After all, no one has bought or sold a slave in the U.S. in well over a century. I think civil rights leaders like Jesse are takers, not leaders."

"Now, no name-calling from our side," Lee said trying to find some humor.

"Well Kelly, this time, the degree to which we simply see the world differently is very obvious," Lynn said looking at Kelly. "I just don't agree. My guess is that we have had different experiences in life and hold onto different views about what America is really like."

"I don't know where you grew up, but I grew up in Chicago," John joined in. "If you were black in Chicago, the rules were different when the police had you in the basement. I came to know some detectives as intimate friends, and they have told me the truth. You may not consider beatings on suspicion of criminal activity to be torture, but Rodney King's experience in LA was not an anomaly. That is the experience of a large number of black Americans."

"When such things happen, they should be confronted *and* changed," Kelly said with feeling.

"Sometimes there have been changes," John admitted. "But often there are not."

"I'm sure our experiences have been different, and I can appreciate your frustration," Kelly continued. "But what one looks for, one can find. I have never expected America to be perfect. I just hope it gets better at living up to the values and freedoms we say we stand for."

"Whites can talk about their values. As black Americans, we talk about behaviors," John countered. "We have to, because we ignore those behaviors at our peril. We are not the dominant culture. White Anglo-Saxon males can afford to believe in values and rights and ignore behaviors. They can ignore discrepancies and experience no consequences. If minorities ignore those discrepancies, they can die for it."

"It may have happened as you say, but it doesn't happen as often now," Lee interjected. "Unfortunately, I think far too many blacks are stuck in the rearview mirror. Even if there are tragic examples of racism and mistreatment, to keep focusing on them does not help them. It leaves blacks angry instead of focused on becoming successful. After all, even if you are right about all the American evils, perpetuating your train of thought creates more cynicism than hope. True hope is not blind to the problems but perseveres anyway in spite of them. Colin Powell always has said that the best revenge for racism was to win anyway."

"That may work for Colin Powell, but it doesn't make it

any easier for the thousands of poor blacks to get ahead in America," John countered.

"Colin Powell is not the *only* successful black American," Lee replied. "How do you explain the success of black Americans who have not been brought up with *black victim* programming?"

"What do you mean?" Lynn asked.

"Blacks of West Indian descent have been able to make the *American Dream* work for them in spite of the color of their skin," Lee explained. "We've already talked about Colin Powell. But what about Sidney Poitier, Harvard sociologist Orlando Patterson, novelist Jamaica Kincaid, the *Enterprise* Publisher Earl Graves—These people are glaring success stories. We aren't talking about just a few people. With over a million blacks of West Indian descent in America, their median income is nearly $10,000 greater than the median income for all black households. They don't seem to buy the myth that the *American Dream* is dead. They haven't been programmed to look to the government; they knew they had to do it the old fashioned way—earn it themselves!"

"Even with affirmative action, people still have to *earn* their success," John said.

"True, but even if they did earn it, it's frequently discounted by others," Lee replied. "That special advantage actually plays into keeping racial bias alive. It is not racism to suggest that the equal protection clause under the obscure and often forgotten U.S. Constitution is still the best policy. It also is still the law of the land."

"That Constitution did not protect black slaves from being slaves," Lynn asserted.

"The blacks that had to endure slavery had a bad hand dealt them, but they are not the only people who have had to learn to play a poor hand well," Lee countered. "Did you see *Gangs of New York?* The Irish had a terrible time. Many of them came to the U.S. in bondage. At one time, half of Philadelphia's population was comprised of white Irish slaves. Now, admittedly, the Irish were slaves for only five years. But that is why they were given all the life-threatening jobs. During war time, the Irish were put in the front lines because it was believed that they liked to fight, and they were expendable. When the Notre Dame sports teams are called *the fighting Irish*, there was a reason. I mention the Irish not to minimize black slavery, but to point out that blacks were not alone in being dealt a poor hand in coming to America."

"I think the movement to have black restitution for slavery is a bad idea," John admitted. "It isn't going to happen. It just adds to the racial tension."

"I agree with you," Lee agreed. "You'd have to start giving money to any group that was wronged. And who would pay—primarily people who have no connection to slavery whatsoever. I would guess that the origins of over 95% of the U.S population began *after* slavery had ended. All of my relatives are Swedish, and they came after the Civil War. Even with the remaining pre-slavery ancestors, by and large, most of their ancestors weren't rich enough to own slaves or were in states that didn't allow them. You can't hold taxpayers liable for those few ancestors who owned slaves."

"There is a class of colored people who make a business of keeping troubles, wrongs, and hardships of the Negro race before the public. Some of these people do not want the Negro to lose his grievances, because they do not want to lose their jobs." –Booker T. Washington

"We agree," Lynn said. "Many blacks we know don't want to push the issue."

"I appreciate that Lynn," Lee confessed. "But if you can see why restitution is not a good idea, you are not too far from seeing why affirmative action may have outlived its usefulness."

"You've made some good points," Lynn confessed.

"A lot of good points," John confessed. "For far too long, our black leaders have been problem finders, not problem solvers. There does seem to be this maddening and growing acceptance of underachievement in our young people. It would truly break Dr. King's heart. While our teens bebop to hip-hop and waste time shucking, jiving and being angry at the white world, other races are widening the gap in education, enterprise, income, and equality. They are living Dr. King's dream."

"Most black Americans are self-reliant, because we have had to be self-reliant," Lynn asserted with pride.

"You're right," Lee said in support. "I read recently that eighty percent of black Americans are now in the middle or upper class."

"But even the strongest among us still crave affirmation. I want that," Lynn continued. "I want it for my children. I want it for all the beautiful, healthy, funny, smart black Americans I have known and loved over the years. I want America to see us in all our complexity, our artfulness, our enterprise, our American-ness. That's the real portrait of black America—that we're strong people, surviving people, capable people."

"It's time to let *that truth* be known," Kelly said. "We need to honor and affirm all those who are making America work. But we have a problem. Republicans think of people as individuals, not as members of any racial, ethnic, or gender group. The Democrats have successfully played to blacks as a group. We have to make sense to the group to reach and gain the trust of the individuals who vote. That isn't easy to do."

"You're making your case to *these* two individuals," Lynn said smiling.

Making a timely entrance, the waiter turned first to Lynn, "Would you like more wine? More water?"

"I don't think I better have any more wine," Lynn said.

"I want to make sure I am still making sense. But I will have some more water. Thank you. The meal is excellent."

"And so is the discussion," Kelly said. "You might want to join in."

"It sounds tempting, but my other tables might object!"

"Understood," Lee replied. "Water all around. Do we need another bottle of wine?"

"OK," John answered.

"One more bottle," Lee said. "I have a feeling the evening is just beginning to get interesting."

"I think you'll make sure of that," Lynn laughed.

Chapter Six

Investing in Affirmative American Examples

"It was my mother and father, who, despite the fact that I was growing up in Jim Crow Alabama, always had me convinced that I could be President of the United States. They always taught me to just look past the obstacles. Either blast through them, or assume they're not in your way.... Growing up where I did in Alabama probably gave me a healthier respect for how far we've come. I don't carry anger about that period of time. I think it made me, and people like me, stronger. I just refuse not to be optimistic. You only have one life. And if you spend your entire life seeing obstacles and seeing clouds and assuming everybody's out to get you, then I think you're just likely to waste your life, and I'm just not going to do that."

—Condoleezza Rice

★ ★ ★

"It isn't just black Americans who are hurt by affirmative action," Lee asserted in between bites.

"You've certainly made it clear that deserving whites have been hurt," John conceded.

"That's true, but those aren't the only people hurt by the allure of affirmative action," John said. "You might have noticed that I have left out other groups—women, Hispanics, gays, and the vast array of other *minority* groups. They are now the people driving for affirmative action. Their activist leaders want a piece of that lucrative entitlement pie. Unfortunately, affirmative action is discrimination no matter how you package it or who you package it for. In fact, for women, there is ample evidence that they are doing fine without it!"

"You are pressing your luck now, Lee," Lynn said laughing. "I'm black *and* a woman."

"I've noticed," Lee answered. "I pick up even subtle cues."

"Boy, are you perceptive!" Kelly added into the levity.

"Don't let me lose my train of thought!" Lee said.

"Ok, just don't let your *train of thought* have a wreck here," Lynn cautioned. "You've been starting to make sense."

"Did you know that women-owned businesses in America employ more workers than all the *Fortune* 500 companies combined?" Lynn asked. "More than 18 million workers."

"No, I did not."

"They are the fastest-growing segment of startup U.S. businesses," Lee continued. "The number of female-owned businesses grew 17% between 1997-2002 compared to just 6% for all U.S. owned firms. Let's face it, the easiest way to break the glass ceiling is to own it. Now, that is Republican all the way. Our bias is in favor of creating wealth, not redistributing wealth because someone says they should get an extra break!"

"It's the same with gay Americans. In our recent economic downturn, gay-tolerant communities still prospered," Kelly added. "As far as I'm concerned, that is good news! It shows the power of the *American Dream*. No matter what the gender, orientation, race or group, Americans can use their freedom, their network and their creative innovation to achieve their share of the dream."

"Even your Log-cabin Republicans have had a hard time finding their place in your party," Lynn said. "I'm surprised to hear of your support."

"While I'm often opposed to the political agenda of the organized homosexual movement, I'm sure I join most Americans from all political parties in celebrating the success of *every* American," Kelly continued. "At the same time, such success argues against the drive to add 'sexual orientation' to equal opportunity protections. When affirmative action was first instituted, black Americans were statistically disadvantaged economically. Homosexuals, on the other hand, make nearly twice the income of the median American worker. We don't need another law to further divide us and protect people who are *already* successful."

"Women and gays may be improving their lot, but what about the Hispanics who the Republicans keep trying to send back to Mexico?" John probed.

"The current obsession with ethnicity and country of origin has ground down to a sterile multiculturalism: the politics of 'difference' without any countervailing politics of 'unity.' What if, instead of thinking about creating yet additional boxes of isolation, we started drawing circles of inclusion? What if, instead of thinking as tribes, we began to behave as one people?"
–Marlene Adler Marks

"I don't think the majority of Republicans want *legal* immigrants from any country to go back to where they came

49

from," Lee cautioned. "We should never forget that most people coming to America do so to aspire to our shared dream of bettering their lives for themselves and their families. They come to assimilate into America by becoming Americans. They come for a better life for their children, and their children's children. We just want to have people come legally."

"Immigration is still a hot issue," Lynn enjoined.

"It's always been a hot issue! The terrorism threats and the increase in illegal immigration just make it hotter," Lee continued. "Bush himself turned up the heat a notch when he announced his guest worker plan. If we get brave, we may want to tackle that later."

"That's a tough one even inside the Republican party," Kelly admitted.

"I agree. For now, let's stay focused on the importance of the *American Dream* for immigrants. We agree on that," Lee continued. "Every age in America seems to worry about waves of immigrants forever changing the heart and soul of what makes America unique. But our motto lives on—*E pluribus Unum*—'out of many one!' Out of the rich mosaic of many ethnic backgrounds we reclaim and reaffirm our commitment to *one* American culture. As I said earlier, I'm a 100% Swedish American, and I have no box on my census to check off. And I don't want one. I love celebrating my heritage, but I am an American first. That's the only box I need on my census. Forget the apostrophes! Let's have one box—*American!*"

"That sure sounds good, but I'm not sure Hispanics share that dream in the same way," John said. "Legal or illegal, many of the Hispanics I know don't seem to want to assimilate."

"That doesn't match the facts that I've read. A study done by Pepperdine University's Institute for Public Policy found that the longer Latino immigrants are in the United States, the more likely they are to latch on to the *American Dream,*" Lee reported. "There seems to be a direct correlation between a Latino immigrant's year of arrival into the United States and his household income. The longer they've lived here, the more they earn and the more likely they are to have mastered English. Legal or illegal, virtually all U.S. born Latinos 16 years-of-age and older are fluent in English. Don't get me wrong, I still feel a need to come up with a plan to deal with illegal immigration, but America still works its magic over time. We come together. We need to make sure we keep coming together."

"You are too optimistic for your own good," Lynn said with a smile. "It's too good to be true."

"True optimism isn't based on Pollyanna thinking," Lee said seriously. "It's based on a track record of overcoming obstacles in pursuit of the dreams you desire. Optimists are usually realists because they really do believe that people can make a difference. That's why people keep coming, because in America they can *still* make their dreams happen."

"Many do," John said.

"Of course they do," Lee agreed. "But the problem is that we don't capitalize on those successes. We don't use them to inspire others. American minorities don't need affirmative action programs; they need a strong dose of *positive gossip* about heroes worth emulating."

"What do you mean?" John asked.

"People like you two," Lee said emphatically. "You are both successful. A strong dose of positive gossip about heroes and achievers from all races and ethnic groups could do wonders in letting those less fortunate know that with strong effort, natural abilities sharpened by education, and a focused dream, *anyone* can be successful. We need models from different races, genders and ages. In this age of cynicism, the Republican Party needs to be a hope merchant that is dedicated to *leaving no American behind!*"

"Do you *really* think that is true?" Lynn asked again.

"More than you might think," Lee continued. "Whatever happens to affirmative action, let's not forget the many affirmative examples who deserve our collective applause. Rosey Grier was one of the LA Rams' *Fearsome Foursome*. He could play football, but, as a minister and community activist after retirement, he wasn't afraid of making some pretty strong statements. I memorized one of them: 'All too often, minority kids never hear about anyone other than athletes. They don't know the living you can make with your mind. When I hear the same thing in black schools as white, kids talking about becoming doctors and lawyers, I know the ghetto will disappear.' I wish I had said that."

"It wouldn't have counted as much if you said it," Kelly said.

"You're right," John confessed. "In this case, it's stronger when a famous black athlete says it. We put sports stars on pedestals, but not our many black business leaders and professionals. You wouldn't know we had any."

"We agree. As far as I'm concerned, it's everyone's responsibility to catch Martin Luther King's dream working," Lee continued. "I'd love to challenge the NAACP *and* the Republican Party to match funds in supporting community service ads doing that very thing. Instead of fighting for special privileges for any group, we ought to be celebrating the millions of minority Americans who have made America work. We ought to be learning from them."

"Would you believe? We are actually in total agreement on something," Lynn said with a smile.

"I told you it would happen," Lee replied. "And there is hope for change. Occasionally positive gossip is even happening. I remember seeing an ABC *20/20* program last year. Kelly, what was that guy's name?"

"Chris Gardner, I think," Kelly answered. "It was inspiring. Chris Gardner went from homelessness in San Francisco to being an owner of a multimillion dollar institutional brokerage firm in the financial district in Chicago, IL."

"Chris himself was inspired by a successful broker. But even in the face of some difficult setbacks, Chris didn't let go of his dream," Lee said, picking up the story. "While trying to care for his young son on the streets of San Francisco, he would spend many a night in the public restroom at a BART rapid transit station. He even had financial help and encouragement from sympathetic prostitutes. But it was the food and shelter supplied complements of Rev. Cecil Williams and the Glade Memorial Church that allowed him to get the time to study and pass his broker exam. The man had two suits that he alternated every day. They never figured out that he was homeless because he was the first to work and the last to leave."

> *"The objective of a generation of civil rights fighters of all races and colors had been to give every American an equal chance at the starting line, but not a guaranteed outcome at the finish line." –Ted Van Dyk*

"That's quite a story," Lynn said.

"Quite a story and *true!*" Lee continued. "He made 200 calls a day. Every time he picked up the phone, he knew he was digging himself out of his hole."

"As a successful executive he still returns to Glade Memorial to donate funds and work the food line," Kelly added. "He speaks to teens and shares an inspiring message—'It's not a black thing or a white thing. It's a green thing. If you can make people money, they don't care what color you are.' I don't know whether he is a Republican, but he sure talks like one. He tells kids that you make your own breaks by studying your books! You don't need to play ball to be a success. To Chris, the big game is played on Wall Street! Chris Gardner is the kind of hope merchant who we all need to support. He is living the dream and deserves all the accolades he is receiving."

"Unfortunately, stories like that rarely get on TV,"

Lee confessed.

"Too rare," Lynn confessed. "It's the criminals, the gangs, and the dope heads who get on the news. OK and all those sports figures you were talking about."

"It shouldn't have to be that way," Kelly replied.

"That's why I vote *Team Republican*," Lee continued.

"You keep trying," Lynn said laughing.

"It's true," Lee continued. "I vote Republican because the party stands for equal opportunity for *all Americans*. Now, it's also our responsibility as a party to prove that we can go beyond words to prove that we can walk the talk."

"It's going to take more than broadcasting a few examples of successful minorities to win over most black Americans," John countered.

"You're right," Lee confessed. "You have to walk the talk over time. Right now, we are crawling the talk, but I think most Republicans would support what I have said."

"Broadcasting successes is just one of the things that needs to happen," John continued. "People search for one, all-purpose answer to our racial tensions. I don't think there is one answer. We'll also need to find ways to do things together—work together, community projects together, any activities that have nothing to do with race! Making a difference together can help break down racial barriers. Over time it will help reduce the self-conscious awkwardness that often comes up when we even try to search for answers."

"It's rare dialogue like this that helps," Lynn interjected. "I really didn't think we could talk so openly about this without a mini-war breaking out."

"Hey, I told you we could do it," Lee said. "That's why Kelly and I are working so hard to convert you lost Democratic souls."

"Oh no, now, we are *lost souls*," John laughed. "It's getting worse!"

"OK, that is a little over the line," Lee confessed smiling. "The German concentration camp survivor, Victor Frankl, once said something I have never forgotten: 'There are only two races, the decent and the indecent.' Once you get to know and trust someone, you don't see the color of their skin. With time, the American melting pot will mix all the races. It's time we take the race and gender cards out of the deck and start living the values we talk about. For me, that means working to support any achieving, responsible man or woman who takes on the responsibilities to match the rights they are given as American citizens. It means continuing to develop friendships with those of backgrounds other than my own. It means doing whatever I can to help *every* responsible American man and woman to take their rightful place in our society, to live in *any* community, to get a quality education, and to work in any job they are qualified to do. When responsible minorities are attacked, it means being one of the first to defend them. I know we still have a long way to go, but I, for one, want to keep and celebrate the progress we have all worked on to achieve."

"That's quite a stump speech. You ought to go into politics," Lynn said. "I might vote for *you.*"

"No, I think I better settle for eating a little more of my dinner before it gets cold," Lee said, brushing off the comment. "I always figure it is important to be informed whether you run or you vote."

"Good idea," John agreed. "You both certainly are informed."

"While we are talking about *lost souls* and difficult issues, I have one for you," Lynn said, looking at Kelly and then Lee. "I have trouble with the Republican stand on abortion."

"I'm so glad you asked," Kelly said. "People say to avoid that topic. I don't think responsible people can. We can talk about that, but let me be frank—not even all Republicans agree on that issue."

"I'm sure it will be food for thought," Lynn said.

"Let's try eating a little more food before it gets cold," Kelly countered. "Lee, you can't keep using your mouth to talk and get any food in there."

"Point taken," Lee confessed. "Think of the calories I am saving."

"Yeah, saving so you have room for dessert," Kelly said. "I know you too well."

Chapter Seven

Abortion: Being a Passionate Centrist

★ ★ ★

"I'm going to shock you, Lynn." Lee said with a smile. "Kelly knows that I wake up every day and give thanks that George W. Bush is President and Bill Clinton is out making millions speaking and playing golf instead of running our country."

"You think that is a shock to me?" Lynn said, shaking her head. "You've made your partisanship quite clear this evening."

"No, that's not the shock," Lee said, as if preparing for a confession. "Please don't strike me dead, God, but I actually think that Bill Clinton was right about something. He said what I think most Americans feel when it comes to abortion, 'Abortion should be safe, legal and rare.'"

"I *am shocked* if that is how you feel," Lynn said, looking at Lee intently. "That's the Democratic platform. Are you sure you wouldn't be shot for saying that in public as a *conser-*

vative, Christian Republican?"

"I wouldn't be alone if I were," Lee said, shaking his head. "I wouldn't be honest if I did not say this is a tough issue for me personally. It is even a tougher problem for our party."

"This is a sensitive area. We can talk about principles that unite us as a party, and I get optimistic when we do," Kelly joined in. "But the Democrats know how to get the Republicans to self-destruct. Two weeks before every election, all they have to do is bring up abortion and Republican unity dissolves. We are our own worst enemies. Abortion is the issue that causes us to eat our own! As a result, Republicans try to avoid it; everybody pleads—'Don't bring up abortion!'"

"Well, you deserve it," Lynn said with passion. "It shouldn't even be in your platform."

"Reluctantly, as the platform now stands, I agree with you," Lee said sadly. "There I've said it. I feel better that my position is out there."

"Reluctantly?" John asked.

"He's reluctant because he knows I don't share that view with him," Kelly said. "It all comes down to a key question to me—What is it that is in the womb? If it's just a 'mass of tissue,' then there is no problem. But if it is truly human, as medical technology and genetic science have proved, then I would love to see them stop this practice. No matter what Roe vs. Wade says, I think it is clearly unconstitutional."

"As you can see, this is a tough issue for our party...and our home," Lee said looking now at John. "Let me get personal with you. Kelly and I have talked about this a lot. We both think abortion is wrong. Abortion on demand, as it now stands, is morally corrupting. It undermines the respect for life. Our son has long flown the coop, but, if by the grace of God, Kelly were to become pregnant again, we'd have the child and call it a blessing."

"You are well off and married," Lynn interjected. "Some

women have fewer options."

"That's true," Kelly said. "But they do have options. There are so many waiting to adopt children who need to be loved. Lynn, personally, could you have an abortion?"

"That's very personal," Lynn said, looking at John and Kelly. "No, I would not have an abortion. I think it's wrong." Lynn paused, wiping a tear with her napkin.

"I'm sorry, Lynn," Kelly said softly. "I didn't mean to..."

"No, it's alright," Lynn said. "My sister had an abortion. I had tried to talk her out of it. It did not go well. It's been difficult for her."

"It's a very emotional issue," Kelly continued. "No matter what we decide or what politicians or judges decide about abortion, no surgical procedure is totally safe. Any abortion is dangerous for the mother, and it's 100 percent lethal for the fetus."

"It's an emotional issue, a moral issue, a religious issue, and, unfortunately, a very difficult political issue," Lee continued. "Lynn, I'm sorry for your sister. But I'm also pretty sure that making abortion illegal would not have changed her mind."

"No, she did not want the child," Lynn said, "She would have gone where she had to in order to get one. As much as I talked about giving the child up for adoption, she felt too guilty to do that."

"What you have gone through with your sister brings home a sharp dose of reality," Lee said. "Whether it is outlawed or an amendment is passed, a woman still has *the choice* whether I like it or not. She can go to where she can have an abortion. So those who support the pro-life position need to devote as much of their attention and their caring for the women with the womb as they do to the child within."

"Absolutely," Lynn said, nodding agreement. "Prohibition doesn't prevent abortion, it just sends it underground. And having more support for having the child might have helped turn my sister from having that abortion."

"It's like parenting," Lee continued. "Once you realize you really don't control your kids' choices, it's better to put all you have into influencing your children to help them make the *right* choice."

"John, I think we are converting them!" Lynn said smiling.

"Now, don't get carried away here," Kelly said. "You have Lee's support, but you don't have mine. And just because I feel a bit outnumbered, that doesn't change the fact that you are talking about choices—choices that could mean the end of a life!"

"The woman has a right to...."

"I know she can choose to end the life of the person in her womb," Kelly continued. "I can't stop her, but I don't want to in any way condone it. Clearly, the right to an abortion is not a Constitutional right. Roe vs. Wade may have given woman that right, but it is a poor decision. I

"The right to obtain an abortion brings with it the responsibility.... With the pro-choice rhetoric we use now, we incur three destructive consequences ... hardness of heart, lying and political failure. By refusing to look at abortion within a moral framework, we lose the millions of Americans who want to support abortion as a legal right but still need to condemn it as a moral iniquity."
—Naomi Wolf

don't know if you know that Case Law has established that the unborn can inherit property, collect Social Security, sue, collect welfare and be the executor of an estate, but suddenly when it comes to the right to life, the unborn are utterly without any rights at all. I know it is a real political problem for the Republicans, but if abortion is unconstitutional and violates our civil rights laws and there are so many inconsistencies in the law regarding the unborn, I think Republicans need to keep on educating and citing medical and scientific evidence. That's why I love the ultra-sound machine—you can see a human being in the womb."

"You don't support any abortion?" Lynn asked, focusing on Kelly.

"I'm against abortion under all circumstances except to save the *life* of the mother," Kelly continued. "I don't support abortion for the health of the mother; that's just too subjective of a reason to end the life of a human being. Abortion, above it all, is a civil rights issue, not a privacy issue or a women's issue."

"This is a hot-button difference for your party," John said. "I can see it in both of your comments here."

"I agree with Lee that it is not and should not be the main political focus for the Republican Party," Kelly continued. "But on the other hand, all other issues that we may be concerned about are meaningless unless we fight and push for the right to life. Whether we get a Constitutional change or just change the hearts and minds of women one woman at a time, we need to care enough to fight that battle."

"Before you think that I've left Kelly to join the Democrats here, I need to clarify my position," Lee said, taking back the focus. "Look, in some ways, it's comfortable to be on the extreme—pro-choice or pro life. For the extremes, your choice is simple. As I have found with Kelly, my position successfully upsets both extremes, but I don't mind being in the middle when I think that it is right. In fact, I'm a passionate centrist on this tough issue, and I don't think I'm alone. There are many Republicans *and* Democrats on both sides of the abortion issue. The recent surveys I have seen put Republican women at close to 50-50 in passion for pro-life and pro-choice. That's Republican women, and we are losing some of those women voters no matter which way we go."

"Will you lose Kelly?" John asked.

"No," Lee said. "Well, maybe I'll let her answer that."

"No, I'm a Republican on principles," Kelly said. "I will vote Republican, but I will be fighting for a stronger push on pro-life than Lee. That's healthy. I won't bolt over this, but I won't be silent."

"You've made some points with me tonight," John answered. "But if Republicans are going to make abortion illegal, Lynn and I would rather stop them than elect them."

"As a man, that doesn't surprise me," Kelly added. "Did you know that more women than men are against abortion? The most pro-abortion support comes from affluent white males. Could it be that they do not want their free sex options to turn into a costly paternity case?"

"I'm not white, and that's not *my reason*," John said, trying to smile.

"No matter how Kelly and I disagree on this, I don't want to get sidetracked. Let's do a little reality testing here," Lee cautioned. "Next week, George W. Bush comes up for reelection after four years in office. Abortion isn't illegal. He said when he took office that he was personally against abortion and felt it was wrong. But he also said that until there is a consensus about what to do on abortion there could be no law or amendment to make abortion illegal. He also made it clear that he will uphold the law, and he has."

"If he had that consensus...." Lynn started.

"Fifty percent of Republicans don't even want to make it illegal," Lee stopped her, "Ronald Reagan was against abortions, but when he was California Governor he signed a permissive abortion bill. He tried to blame his decision on doctors who he said deliberately misrepresented the law. I think he knew what he was doing; it's a tough issue. Now, when he ran for President, he advocated a Constitutional Amendment that would have prohibited all abortions except when necessary to save the life of the mother. But at pro-life rallies, he would telephone in a message. Some said that he didn't want pictures with the leaders to be seen on the evening news. This is nothing against Ronald Reagan. I respect him immensely, and I don't doubt his sincerity. But abortion was not his focus; he knew there was no consensus. There still is no consensus. It should not be our party's focus now! And, *it isn't* our party's focus!"

"But what about the ban on partial-birth abortion?" John asked.

"There we have had consensus," Kelly said. "Most Americans have no stomach for supporting late-term abortions or the partial-birth procedures they often use. In fact, they have never felt comfortable making abortion too easy to get. In most states, there is also support for a 24-hour delay, parental or judicial involvement, and programs to help prospective mothers consider other choices. These aren't extreme positions."

"After what you said, Kelly, I'm afraid that these *far right* laws will just fuel demands for making abortion illegal." Lynn countered.

"I must confess that I would like that," Kelly said. "But I also realize that my position is not the most popular one in the party."

"Every time Bush has called for an end to partial-birth abortions, Democrats love to label it a 'far right position,'" Lee sited. "But Gallup polls have supported that as many as 70 percent of Americans back the law to bar it. That doesn't make it *far right*. Even the American Medical Association has been unsupportive of partial-birth abortion. With all that modern medicine has to offer, partial birth abortion is never needed to save the life or health of a mother."

"There is widespread consensus for some common sense limits," Kelly added. "Most schools require a signed consent form on file before schools will dispense an aspirin to a young woman, yet current abortion laws in many states allow that same young women to have an abortion without even notifying parents. They want parents to have no say, but they expect the parents to pick up the emotional pieces and pay the bills when the child suffers physical or emotional damage as a result of that abortion. You can't support that, can you?"

"You and I both know that physical damage is rare, and, let's face it, some parents don't even want to talk to their kids," Lynn interjected.

"We realize that, but these limits are not extreme. Here, Kelly and I agree. If the parents won't talk, the young woman can present her case to a judge," Lee continued. "Even cultures in Europe that have had long-standing support for abortions have worked to provide delays, counseling and clear consideration of other options for women making the choice. Take the French model. Take the Swedish model and make me happy as a Swedish American. All of them treat this not as a woman's rights issue, but as a difficult choice that ought to be done early, with time to think, and with encouragement to have the child unless the woman is under extreme distress. They don't condone abortion as just another birth control method. They influence women to keep the child, not terminate the fetus. I mean, how many times do you find Europe being more conservative than America on any issue? In America, the norm in abortion is—'You want it, you get it!' The feminists just try to make an issue of a woman's right to choose. It's her body; it's her choice! That's always bothered me. A woman may have the right to do anything she wants with her body, but this isn't her body. It's *in* her body."

"I'm glad you said that," Kelly added. "I'm glad they make them take time to think, but I would argue that 'extreme distress' should never be an excuse for intentionally killing a growing child. If it is, then abortion is, tragically, the planned death of another human being to solve the stress problems of someone else."

"But abortions are allowed in France?" John asked.

"Yes, but just because it is allowed in Europe, doesn't mean that abortions are approved in those countries," Lee jumped in. "They can make the choice, but it can't be done lightly. In America, they try to make it simply a woman's choice issue.

They don't want anything to do with the guilt of the pain involved in making this tough decision. Don't make me even wait 24 hours or it's a hardship. I think the French require a week."

"You don't think women in America feel guilt?" Lynn countered. "Guilty or not, women still need the right to make that choice."

"You may think Kelly is extreme, but the pro-abortion extremists can also go too far," Lee asserted. "Once contraception has failed, the woman has all the rights; she alone has the right to get an abortion. But if she decides to have the child, she can make the father pay support, whether he wanted it or not. His interest becomes relevant only when the mother wants money to support her choice. They want total responsibility only when it suits them. Other interests ought to be taken into account."

"Whose interests?" John asked before Lynn could.

"It's not just a woman's rights issue," Lee answered. "What about the man whose sperm created the developing fetus? What about a society that is concerned about future generations and the values that sustain that culture? What about the developing life in her womb? If any of these have a right to be considered in any decision, then it is more than a woman's rights issue. In fact, even if an abortion is chosen for very valid and difficult reasons, it is still a tragedy. Unfortunately, as far as I'm concerned, neither extreme accepts the tragedy if they fully win the war on abortion. If a developing life is not allowed to reach its potential, it's a tragedy. If a woman is forced to have an unwanted child and does not have the options or the support to raise it well or give it up for adoption, it's tragedy. If they can't see the tension involved in this tough choice, they are part of the problem. Not resolving that argument puts me squarely in that passionate middle."

"We had a speaker on abortion at our Republican Women Federated meeting. More and more states are passing common sense restrictions on abortion," Kelly said. "Nearly 20 states require a waiting period, 25 have state-directed counseling, over 30 require a minor to get permission or to notify a parent before having an abortion. Maryland is among a shrinking number of states where laws are still lenient; they have few if any restrictions. In Maryland, the abortion rate is twice as high as it is in Pennsylvania where the laws are strict. To me, that's living proof that stricter laws can work. It doesn't go far enough for me, but it is an important step."

"I'm just afraid the right to abortion is hanging in tenuous balance," Lynn said. "Roe vs. Wade is just one Supreme Court justice's vote away from being overturned. Today's women too easily take abortion rights for granted. For young women in college now, hearing about a time without abortion is like hearing about Prohibition. I think no matter how many stories you hear about women using knitting needles and hangers, when you grow up in a generation that has access to abortion, you cannot even imagine it."

"Let's not talk about knitting needles and hangers just yet," Lee countered. "The pro-abortion crowd would have you believe that thousands died from such back-alley abortions, but in 1972, one year before the Roe vs. Wade ruling, less than 40 women died from illegal abortions."

> *"When we talk about abortion, we are talking about two lives — the life of the mother and the life of the unborn child. Why else do we call a pregnant woman a mother? I have also said that anyone who doesn't feel sure whether we are talking about a second human life should clearly give life the benefit of the doubt. If you don't know whether a body is alive or dead, you would never bury it. I think this consideration itself should be enough for all of us to insist on protecting the unborn."* –Ronald Reagan

"That's 40 too many!" Lynn countered.

"One is too many, but think of how many babies never were given the chance to see life," Kelly added again. "When abortion was illegal in the U.S., as it was in most of the states before Roe vs. Wade came down, the woman was usually considered a victim under the law. It was the abortionist, not the woman, who was prosecuted. I believe today that the women who have abortions are still the victims—victims of misinformation and plain lies about what they have growing in their bodies. They aren't even informed about the risks, both physical and psycho-emotional, from abortion. Think of your sister."

"My sister's experience is not every woman's experience," Lynn responded. "I don't want to limit their choices."

"A woman's choice is not limited to what the Supreme Court does," Lee said. "When the U.S. Supreme Court handed down its historic decision legalizing abortion, abortion was legal in some states. The Roe vs. Wade decision just overruled laws against abortion in states which barred the procedure. And so, if Roe vs. Wade were overturned, the ability to regulate abortion would return to the states and though many would maintain or impose limitations, undoubtedly, abortion would remain legal in many states, even more states than before. As much as Kelly and others might want it, I really don't think any amendment will ever pass."

"I agree with you," John said. "Roe vs. Wade was a state's rights ruling. That being said, even *conservative* justices take precedent seriously. The longer Roe vs. Wade is not reversed, the safer it is. At the same time, I agree that some limits do make sense. But Kelly, when young women are called 'murderers' by right-to-life advocates, they leave me and others reluctantly stuck having to defend the right of women to make this tough choice."

"I understand," Kelly said. "But who is standing up for the rights of the unborn. Don't you feel a need to defend their rights? I don't like to see pro-life demonstrators screaming at women going into clinics either."

"Some of them don't just scream," Lynn added. "They kill abortion doctors. They put 'Wanted' posters with abortion doctors' pictures on websites. They list names and addresses."

"That is rare, but it does happen. I don't condone it," Kelly confessed. "In fact, outside of a few extremists the media loves to catch defending the killers, the *overwhelming* majority of pro-life loyalists and groups have condemned those actions. When they caught Eric Rudolph rummaging for food in a dumpster, the vast majority of Christians applauded that he was finally caught and held responsible. No matter what you feel about pro-life protestors, there has been a decline in the number of violent attacks on clinics."

"You're Christians," John continued. "Is it killing to you?"

"Can't we hide behind separation of church and state?" Lee said with hesitation.

"Not at *this* dinner," Lynn said. "You set the rules to talk openly."

"I think Lee and I both feel it is wrong to not give life a chance." Kelly interjected. "As Lee said earlier, if I became pregnant, we would have the child and figure out how to handle it later."

"At our age, that would be an adventure," Lee said. "But we'd have the child."

"Is it killing?" John asked again.

"One death is a tragedy," Kelly said. "A million abortions per year is a statistic without faces. We can't handle a million faces that are never seen, so we hide in the statistics. I will *never* be comfortable with easy abortions and the lives that never had a chance to be lived. To me it is killing."

"You can't minimize a million abortions. The sanctity of life is so critical, but I don't think killing a person is the same as an abortion," Lee said thoughtfully. "Dennis Prager has helped me a lot on this issue. He's a moral thinker, a religious Jew and radio talk show host. He clarifies things so well. He helped me find a new understanding about the Biblical perspective. He's the first to admit that the issue of when life begins will always be debated and should be debated, but that his understanding of Scripture helps him accept the difference between a fetus and a newborn baby. The word in Hebrew for 'breathe' and 'soul' are the same. That is why an argument can be made from a Judeo-Christian perspective that true life begins at the moment of birth when a baby first fills its lungs with air. He points out that, in Exodus 21:22-23, the punishment for a man who causes a miscarriage is less severe than for killing the woman."

"That is not permission to sanction abortions," Kelly said interrupting.

"You're right," Lee continued. "This should not be used as a defense of abortion on demand, but it does affirm that men of faith can assert that there is a difference between killing a live baby and aborting a fetus. If Biblical perspectives don't matter to you, he asks some important questions that pro-life advocates need to ask themselves: If abortions were illegal, would you agree to put the mother to death or in prison for life for having that abortion? Should we execute doctors who perform abortions as we do mass murderers? If your answer to either of these questions is 'no,' you too do not see having an abortion as morally indefensible as killing a live baby or another person."

"Those are powerful questions that I don't think many people ask themselves," John said thoughtfully.

"I have," Kelly said. "Lee has asked me. As I said before, the woman should not be prosecuted for murder. The doctor should be held accountable. It's not the same as murder, but there should be a severe punishment and prosecution."

"I didn't realize that women were not prosecuted," Lynn said. "That's good to know."

"A lot who feel like I do will never soften their position," Kelly continued. "Many care so much about this issue that they fear calm arguments are not enough. They take an extreme position to shock people. They want them to know that what they are doing is bad. When I hear about woman having an abortion instead of having it interfere with a planned vacation, I want to scream too. I'd like to grab a lot of people in America and say, 'Aren't you upset that our culture terminates a million developing lives and acts like it's just a simple choice?'"

"That's the problem," Lynn reacted. "People feel *too strongly.*"

"Strong moral discussions are needed on the abortion issue and shouldn't be stopped," Lee said. "William Bennett and others have challenged Republicans to establish a workable position on abortion that stresses influence instead of legal control. Instead of mounting a battle on the legal and political arena, they have to make their case on moral grounds. In the messy and flawed world we live in, we ought to be fighting for a way to revive a moral awareness where fewer women choose death of the fetus over giving that fetus life. I join those who feel that we need to stop supporting an unattainable human life amendment and start working to influence the culture that has worked hard to make abortion just another lifestyle decision for a woman."

"You don't sound like a Republican!" Lynn stressed.

"Not so," Lee countered. "As a conservative who believes in the limited role of government, it is important for right-to-life advocates to be willing to consider limitations on their own power! I do not want coercive control from the extreme right or control from the extreme left on this important issue. Let's have leaders who at least try to stop unwanted pregnancies and who actually campaign to give women more options that will help avoid abortions."

"Republicans still stress the right-to-life, and that won't go away," John said.

"It shouldn't go away!" Kelly joined in. "I never want

Republicans to be pro-abortion. That's what the pro-choice extremists have become. Some don't even want to call the developing child a fetus; some prefer just 'uterine material.' It's not aborting a fetus; it's terminating a pregnancy or exercising reproductive choice. We speak of killing weeds and cockroaches, but a developing child, growing, or even kicking inside you? It's not 'alive' enough to kill. I would welcome a leader who would use the Presidential bully pulpit to talk forcefully in support of abstinence, adoption, crisis pregnancy centers, and individual responsibility. In fact, I think Bush is that kind of President. I would rather have a Republican team in power in Washington talking about keeping abortions rare. And as much as I understand that this is not popular, I think pro-life demonstrators should be allowed the same rights of expression as any other American is allowed. With some recent court reversals, the sidewalks in front of abortion clinics will remain open to free speech and free discourse. They can't block the entrances but they need to be free to influence mothers making this difficult decision."

"Free speech is one thing, but a call for an abortion amendment doesn't belong in the Republican platform, either state or national," John said. "I have never understood how Republicans can propose on one hand more government intervention in that very personal issue while on the other hand urging government to get out of people's lives."

"Join the party, John," Lee countered. "Then you can work to make that case for change."

"You're sneaky," John laughed.

"Seriously, I could use your help." Lee continued. "I don't think even Kelly would complain."

"RU 486 is going to make this whole issue irrelevant," Lynn said assertively. "Women won't have to wait to have an abortion. The morning after pill is going to be even more available."

"I think you may be right," Kelly replied. "But it's not as

71

simple as it sounds in the newspapers. It's still a complicated and lengthy process with a minimum of three visits to the doctor's office. I've read that up to 5 percent end up still needing surgery at the end of the process. I just hope women don't use RU 486 as an excuse to not take responsibility for their sexual choices."

"I hope not, too," Lynn confessed. "But it's still their choice."

"I consider it a lousy birth control *choice,* and using it indiscriminately is against all that I hold dear," Kelly continued. "But even though I do not condone abortions, would not have one, and would be disheartened if a daughter of mine had one, I realized that, ultimately, that decision must be made by a woman, hopefully in consultation with the father, her doctor, her minister, and her God."

"No matter what we say here, the number of abortions is decreasing," Lynn continued. "I've read that the U.S. abortion rate has been on a consistent decline since 1980."

"A million abortions a year is still too many," Lee added. "But you win this battle one heart at a time, and every heart is worth that fight whether it's the woman who makes the choice or the developing child not yet born."

"After this conversation, it is clear that Republicans don't agree on this?" John asked.

"You're right," Kelly said. "That's why both Lee and I are sensitive to the strongly held opinions of many in our party who would disagree. As a result, we are strongly against forcing people to pay taxes that go to support abortions they abhor. There is no Constitutional right for abortion. I just expect clinics to raise the funds to support their efforts. We shouldn't involve government funds."

"I could agree with that, if the right to an abortion stays legal," Lynn affirmed.

"Don't worry," Kelly said. "I listen to a lot of politicians talking to women. Most avoid the abortion issue. They want the issue to go away, but it won't go away until it is faced. The smart ones state their position early. They limit it to a 15 second sound byte and then move on to issues women care even more about—issues like educating their children."

"Education is important," Lynn agreed.

"I feel a new topic coming on," John said.

"Thankfully," Lee said. "I think we survived."

"This is a lot of words to digest," John said.

"Enough said. Let's trade digesting these words, for finishing our entrees," Kelly said.

"Sounds like a good idea," John agreed.

"Thank you both for talking about this," Lynn said with appreciation. "It's been helpful *and* strangely reassuring. It seems like consensus on abortion is a long way from being resolved in either party. It just felt good to talk openly about it."

Chapter Eight

Educational Excellence Means Leave No One Behind

"Is there a gap between the rich and the poor in America? The answer is no. The gap is quite different. There is growing gap between people with advanced education and people without. The difference in income for an Afro-American with a college degree is statistically insignificant (if you adjust for age and length of service) from the income of a white, Latino, or Asian with a college degree. The gap is almost 100 percent educational." –Peter Drucker

★ ★ ★

"When it comes to our challenge in education, Bush sums it up pretty well—'Leave no child behind!' Ignorance is dangerous not only to our children but to our way of life," Lee said confidently.

"You don't have a monopoly on this passion, John F. Kennedy said it differently 40 years ago, 'The ignorance of one voter in a democracy impairs the security of all,'" John added. "I don't think any American would disagree with either message. We all want the best for our children. We just disagree on how to accomplish that."

"Agreed!" Kelly said. "Everybody knows that the shortest and surest way from poverty to wealth is a good education."

"You talk about lectures we received as kids," Lynn said with a smile. "There's an old Haitian proverb my mother loved to tell me over and over again: 'Ignorance doesn't kill you, but it makes you sweat a lot.' I didn't like sweating a lot. I followed her advice and worked hard at school."

"I think my mom went to the same parent lecture training!" Lee said. "But she kept quoting Benjamin Franklin, 'We are all born ignorant, but one must work hard to remain stupid.' She was sure I was working *very hard* at being stupid!"

> *"I would say to a black boy what I would say to the white boy, 'Get all the mental development that your time and pocketbook will allow of.'"*
> *–Booker T. Washington*

"That's a good one!" John said, joining the laughter.

"But with all this common commitment to education we still are not succeeding in our schools," Kelly countered. "I remember reading about a New York State teacher of the year who once said, 'School is a twelve-year jail sentence where bad habits are the only curriculum truly learned.' And that was the *best* teacher saying that!"

"That may be a bit of an overstatement," Lynn asserted.

"I'm not so sure. The American education establishment and the *Democrats* who have been the recipients of their lobbying funds and support have just made things worse," Lee countered. "They have consistently made school easier and cut the competition for excellence to increase student self-esteem. In California, they keep asking for more money and more bonds when we already spend over $7,000 per student. What's it gotten us? Our results in California consistently put us near the bottom of all the states. They work to limit any reference to God or morals while supporting any politically correct cause they can find."

"I *sense* you don't like our public schools too much!" Lynn said with a wry smile.

"You are perceptive," Lee said. "I'm sorry. I do get a bit carried away. I'm just frustrated. We aren't getting the excellence for our kids that they deserve! It's affecting their future."

"There are some good public schools!" Lynn claimed with mild enthusiasm.

"Of course," Kelly said. "There are many great teachers as well. Do you send your children to public schools?"

"No, we don't," John said, jumping in. "It's not an entirely comfortable subject. Lynn would rather have them in public school. I want them to get the best education they can get, and we can afford it."

"You are not alone," Lee said with understanding. "If we had not had good public schools, we would have done the same. That's why it bugs me when Democrats keep fighting school choice and vouchers. When Clinton, Gore and Jesse Jackson were in Washington, they all sent their kids to private schools. And they're not alone. Nationally, roughly ten percent of parents send their kids to private schools. But in Washington, nearly half of the U.S. Senators and almost a third of the U.S. Representatives send their kids to private schools. Do you think that says something about their confidence in public schools?"

"Clinton is gone. Republicans have the White House, Congress, *and* the Senate," John said. "I don't see any glowing changes."

"I think we have seen some changes, but more changes are needed," Lee said. "Instead of lowering standards to support the self-esteem of poor performers, they are doing what they can to raise standards, to test for competence and to fight for school choice where states want to try vouchers."

"Now, kids are spending all of their time learning irrelevant facts in order to pass tests," Lynn said. "There has been *no* dramatic turnaround, and they are flunking more kids than they are helping. Have you been reading about all the kids that are not graduating because they can't pass a high school graduation test?"

"The Federal No Child Left Behind Act that passed in 2001 didn't mandate a test for high school graduation," Lee clarified. "But it did require all schools to implement standards and annual tests in reading and math for students in grades three through eight. And those schools had to show 'adequate yearly progress,' not only for the school, but for minority groups."

"That doesn't help those kids that are flunking out of high school," Lynn continued.

"I don't blame the kids and the parents for being upset," Kelly added. "It isn't fair! They were told a lie. Their schools failed to teach them to read. They gave them good grades they didn't deserve; they kept promoting them when they weren't ready. They should feel cheated. We ought to hold those schools as accountable as we have those kids."

"There's still no dramatic turnaround," John replied.

"Turnarounds take time," Kelly said. "You don't change a system over night, especially a system that fights change."

"Only time will tell, but I can tell you what Republicans will *try to do* to make education work for our kids," Lee said with feeling.

"Alright, I'm listening," John said. "And will raise my hand when I need a bathroom break."

"You'll stay in your seat until *the lesson* is over!" Lee said, feigning anger.

"I think he means it!" Lynn said, joining in the fun.

"Seriously, it all starts with an attitude," Lee stressed. "We have to raise the expectations of our kids instead of worrying about their fragile self-esteem. Good teachers care enough to have high standards. If we were lucky, we each had teachers like that. They wouldn't put up with what kids get away with today."

"You've got that right!" Lynn laughed. "I had teachers who could put the fear of God in you with a stare!"

"And, it didn't hurt you did it?" Lee said, looking straight at Lynn. "In high school, I had *Mrs. Mason*. She was one of those teachers kids warned you *not to get*! I remember, 'Oh, no! You've got Mrs. Mason!'"

"He's telling the truth," Kelly said. "I met her at one of his early reunions. She was still a little scary."

"She was special, so don't say anything bad about Mrs. Mason," Lee said, requesting a little respect. "I had done well in English, but no one had pushed me. I was far more interested in football and just wanted to get through my senior year. My first paper for her I did the night before it was due. When I got it back, there were red marks all over it. I turned to the last page, a 'C-'. I had never even had a 'C' in English. I thought maybe she had had a bad day."

"He was arrogant even then," Kelly added her wifely perspective.

"Careful now, I thought I was better than I was," Lee said. "Hey, I was no more arrogant than today's kids. You've seen those studies in the papers. Today, our kids have the *highest* self-esteem of any of the industrialized countries, but they have the *worst* performance in math and science. She didn't let me get away with that; she cared enough to put me in my place."

"What did you do?" Lynn asked.

"I waited until after class. I went up to her," Lee said, now laughing to himself. "I didn't know how to say it. She put me out of my misery when she said with a smile, 'You're not used to this. Are you Mr. Sanders?' After confessing that I was used to getting better grades in English, she put in the hook and yanked hard—'Your potential shows, but this paper looks like you did it last night.'"

"She knew," Lynn said laughing.

"It probably wasn't hard to figure out. The paper was *not good*," Lee confessed, but stopping the laughter with his upraised hand. "She wasn't done! She said, 'I'm not going to let you get away with this. I expect more from you on your next paper. In fact, I will grade you harder, because I think you our capable of being a good writer.'"

"Today you could hire a lawyer and win!" John joined in. "I could see the headlines—'Teacher Loses Job for Unfair Demands!'"

"Mrs. Mason wasn't afraid to push students!" Lee continued. "I'm sure I wasn't the only one she said that to, and she cared enough to raise the bar on all of us. I worked my tail off in her class my senior year. She brought the best out in me. I *earned* my 'A' in that class."

"We don't have enough Mrs. Mason's to go around," Lynn said. "And if we did, they certainly don't want to teach in the inner city."

"Look hard enough, and you'll find some. Tough teachers come in all colors and in all schools," Lee added.

"Easy to say," John said. "You are sounding like a politician."

"Have you heard about Helen Carithers, an inner-city school teacher at Benjamin Mays High in southwest Atlanta?" Lee asked.

"No, should I have?" Lynn asked.

"Mrs. Carithers is another Mrs. Mason, and she knows the importance of challenging students," Lee continued. "Mrs. Carithers expects *all* her children to achieve. She believes that when kids have high expectations, they will meet those expectations. She takes it as a personal affront that black students who were accepted by colleges like Harvard, MIT, Princeton had to go to summer remedial programs to be ready to be freshmen. She took it upon herself to make sure that *her students* were prepared to go to any school in the nation. Her students from Mays don't need *remedial work!*"

"A rare teacher," Lynn said.

"That is sadly true, but if Mrs. Carithers and Mrs. Mason can get excellence, more teachers can," Lee said. "I remember one of Mrs. Carithers' quotes. She said, 'Some say the SAT is racist. I say the SAT is preparation. The SAT is the name of the game, and we have to go out and play the game.' Her kids may not make the NBA, but they will win at the game of life."

"That's *THE* game!" Lynn said. "I wonder if cloning would be possible with these teachers?"

"I wish such attitudes were an infectious disease!" Kelly said.

"If we make people famous for the right reasons, maybe it can be a bit more infectious. I do know this—if we start requiring high goals in our schools, those attitudes will be more prevalent. When you're playing a tough game to win, people play harder!" Lee continued. "If I'm just shooting baskets, it's lay back time. But if someone says, 'Let's play to twenty-one; loser pays,' we have a game!"

"Got that right," John said, laughing. "That is when old men pull muscles!"

"We have to have a few more teachers and students pulling a few more *mental* muscles because they have to win the game," Lee said. "That's why Bush and his people keep pushing for national standards and tests. With accountability, you have to let go of all the excuses and push for performance."

"*As we go into the twenty-first century, there is nothing more important to bring as an asset than one's mind. It is the single most important piece of capital for the twenty-first century—a trained mind. If you don't have it, you're going to be left behind.*"
—William Bennett

"It can be brutal," Lynn said. "They are failing a lot of kids just because they can't pass tests."

"That isn't the pressure that counts!" Lee asserted. "When you are given a test at work and you fail, you don't get the job. That is real life pressure."

"I remember a bank manager who I met at a conference," Kelly added. "She said that they couldn't find tellers who could even pass the basic English test that they required. So they put together a course for people who wanted to learn what they needed to pass the teller exam."

"Did they get their tellers?" John asked.

"No, that was the really frustrating thing," Kelly confessed. "By the time they got the training and could pass, they had skills that allowed them to get better jobs. None of them wanted to be tellers."

"Oh, that's bad," Lynn said, shaking her head.

"This can't continue if we are to be successful as a country," Lee said. "That's why achievement testing is so important. We need *some* consistent standard so that people have to stretch."

"We already have the SAT's," John said.

"That comes after the war is already lost," Kelly said. "You need more frequent tests so you can catch problems quicker."

"Don't get me started on the SAT," Lee added. "Since the 1960s, the spending on education is up well over 200%, but SAT scores have declined nearly 30%."

"I thought there was more improvement than that," John added.

"In recent years, papers have reported marginal increases in SAT scores for American students, but the meaning of that increase must be kept in perspective," Lee continued. "SAT grading was made easier in 1996. With SAT scores in 1996, a score of 500 on verbal would be 428 on the previous year's scale. That's the problem, most improvements are a mirage. In the real world, the bar is always being raised. In the educational world, it keeps getting lowered. Do you see a problem with that?"

"I do," John said. "I did not realize those scores had been

lowered. Makes me feel better about the scores I had."

"Me, too," Lynn said.

"National education standards establish what students need to know and what they need to be able to do by the time they graduate to the next grade level," Kelly added. "That means there are fewer surprises for high school kids who are not competent enough to graduate. It also insures an easier transfer from school to school. It doesn't mandate how to reach those standards, but it gives them the next bar they need to get over."

"Teachers don't like being controlled," Lynn said.

"Their political donations to the Democratic party help prove that. But let me assure you that when American children are achieving, they'll get the support they want!" Lee said. "Until then, Republicans are pretty clear. We don't want to over-control teachers. We want to free them to achieve results. We want more local control, but we also want to see results. With any luck, they'll stop complaining and start learning from the Mrs. Masons and Mrs. Carithers who are out there!"

"I hope you're right," Lynn said sympathetically.

"We need to do more than set standards and give tests," Lee said. "We need to let states experiment with vouchers and school choice. Every parent ought to be empowered to get the best schooling for their children. You can't do that in a monopoly where you are forced to send your children to a bad school."

"Vouchers will drain needed money from the very schools that need it most," Lynn said.

"That's what the Democrats and the National Education Association want you to believe," Lee said. "They keep saying it will destroy American education. Senator Ted Kennedy all but said that when he said that school choice would be, and I quote, 'a death sentence for public schools struggling to serve disadvantaged students, draining all good students out of poor schools.' It almost sounds like he *wants to keep* our kids in *poor schools!*"

"The NEA is just as bad," Kelly added. "One of their

presidents said that 'Free market economics works well for breakfast cereals, but not for schools in a democratic society. Market-driven school choice would create an inequitable, elitist educational system.' We allow that now for those who can afford it."

"Competition works. It works in colleges and in pre-schools where some parents have choices in using government funds," Lee said, "Note, with some pride, that school choice is working in Sweden. That land of liberals has gone to vouchers because it works. Limited programs are working in some states and cities. Where state voters will support it, vouchers should be given a chance. We need to see what it can do to improve education in America."

> *"Every time we touch a public school and open it up to the marketplace for bidding, we drive up the quality and drive down the price. Competition always creates efficiencies."*
> *–Stephen Goldsmith*

"California has already rejected vouchers," John said.

"That's true, but it was a poorly written proposition," Lee confessed. "And the teacher lobby invested heavily in defeating it."

"It would lose again, if they tried," Lynn said.

"We may have to wait for other states who are motivated to try it to show us the way," Kelly added. "If they get results, others will follow. Maybe even California."

"If California won't go for a full-fledged voucher system, I'd love to see the state at least have a voucher system *within* the public schools," Lee went on. "Allow parents to enroll their children in *any* public school that meets their students' needs. They do that in colleges and universities, why not K-12? The faculty in higher education has a union, too, but they also teach in universities that have to compete for customers! The students are the *customers*, and their choices direct where the public dollars go. Parents should be able to do the same thing in the lower grades."

"There may be more choices and better transportation out here, but not in the inner city," Lynn added. "Getting to *any* school is not a realistic option."

"Let those who want that choice and are willing to work to exercise it, have that choice!" Kelly asserted. "If it worked for their children, more parents would find a way to get their kids in a good school. Now, they are just trapped. You know that surveys indicate that many poor Americans are the biggest supporters of vouchers, but the Democrats will have none of it."

"With less money for the public schools, those schools will lose what good teachers they have," Lynn stressed.

"I think that is what teachers fear," Lee said. "But it's an irrational fear. School choice will put the pressure where it belongs, not on increasing district budgets and funding lobbying efforts in Sacramento and Washington but on getting a better education from the funds we have already committed."

"It will be tough on teachers," Lynn continued. "They are already poorly paid."

"That's the fear, but, if you are good, they should do better in a market-oriented system," Lee said.

"Why?" Lynn asked.

"It's simple really," Lee continued. "Most parents would want to stay in the school that is near them. Most would not leave, but the school would know that they *might* leave. Now, if you are a district administrator and you know you are competing for students and the funds they represent, would you want good teachers or bad teachers?"

"That is simple," Lynn laughed. "Good teachers."

"Added funds today just seems to produce more bureaucracy, not more help where it is needed—in the classroom in the form of good teachers," Lee continued. "But if you have to keep students, you get rid of the bad teachers, and you make sure you keep your best teachers. They will pay them *well*, because *good teachers* produce *good students*, and that is where the money will be. Parents will move their kids to where schools are working. Teachers have nothing to fear unless they are not good teachers."

"In a system with an abundance of schools, vouchers might work," John entered the conversation. "There just aren't enough schools to make this work."

"Those schools will be created," Lee asserted. "There weren't initially enough wireless phone options; now there are hundreds. Markets respond to demands. New schools will start; good ones will grow and remain."

"Having parents choose any public school might work," Lynn countered. "But some vouchers will be used for religious schools. Separation of church and state should be upheld!"

"I think we have gone way too far in bashing religion," Kelly said. "Our founding Fathers wanted to insure freedom *of religion* not freedom *from religion*! Grants and loans can be used at religious colleges and universities. With school vouchers, parents would be given the right to apply those funds in any school, secular or religious, as long as they meet national standards of educational accountability. As a Christian, I am more than pleased to allow public funds to go for any Jewish or Islamic family who cares enough to have their children raised with an appreciation of their own faith. We have negated the value of faith in excellence and in fostering moral development. It's time we realize that arguing over moments of silence in public schools is not the real issue. The real issue is—Are we preparing our youth to appreciate the value of education, moral values, and faith? Vouchers will allow Americans of faith to affirm that appreciation."

"Many Americans have no faith," Lynn said.

"American atheists can use their vouchers where they want," Kelly said. "They can certainly find plenty of public schools where their lack of faith will be protected. After all, if secular academics are so sure students do not need God, prayer, and structure in their lives, they can put their kids where their mouths are. Just don't make the rest of Americans suffer along with them."

"You've made a good case," John confessed. "I know many of my friends are frustrated with the Democratic position on vouchers. I just am not sure school choice will be as effective as people think."

"Choice with vouchers may not be the perfect answer, but it should be tested," Lee agreed. "Like many Americans, with the job that schools are doing, I vote against any bond issue asking for more money for schools. Things have to change. I wouldn't impose vouchers on everyone; I just hope that we can give it a good test somewhere. Some good old, controlled capitalism in education just might work wonders."

"So that's the Republican position," Lynn continued. "High expectations, student testing and vouchers?"

"That's the heart of the platform as far as I'm concerned," Lee said. "But I'd like to see more. Schools don't need more money; they need fewer administrators. Some district budgets invest over half of their funds in administrative costs and special programs. When corporations face difficult times, they cuts administrative costs and levels; they invest only on things that make a difference to their customers. Too many districts leave the levels of administration untouched and then claim that there is nothing for teachers and no books for the students. That burns me! If any district can't keep administrative costs at an established level, they ought not to be given federal or state funds."

"Some of those special programs are for mandated programs for special needs children," Lynn countered. "That is expensive, and it isn't going away."

"I see no difficulty in agreeing to additional voucher support for legitimate special needs children," Lee added. "But they still ought to be able to go to programs that work. Everyone seems to have ADD nowadays, and they all want special programs. I think there is some abuse here, but there is some legitimate need as well."

"Administrators don't change easily," John said.

"Few monopolies ever do," Lee confessed. "New York's public schools have more than ten times as many administrators per student as the city's Catholic schools. Vouchers could help change that in any city. If you have to keep students and control costs, you will cut what doesn't add value. But, even without vouchers, leaders can make a difference. You remember Mrs. Carithers?"

"How could we forget!" Lynn said with a smile.

"John Falco in East Harlem School District is another one of those unsung educational giants we need to honor," Lee continued. "Under his leadership, that district went from the worst to one of the best by eliminating bureaucracy, letting teachers run their own schools, and by forcing schools to compete for students. They gave parents a say in curriculum and standards, and then he kept them involved. He again proved that an inner-city neighborhood need not limit educational excellence."

"Everybody hates to waste money," John confessed.

"Some say that but don't act that way," Lee countered. "They waste money, because we allow them to do that and still get more funds."

"You said there were a couple of things you'd stress more if you were king for a day," Lynn said.

"I don't think I put it that way, but there is one more thing," Lee said, pausing for the right way to introduce it. "UCLA's great basketball coach John Wooden used to say, 'It is what you learn after you know it all that counts.' George Bush talks about leaving no child behind, but I would go further. We can't afford to leave any American behind no matter at what age they need to learn new marketable skills."

"We can hardly afford what we spend on our kids," John said. "And now you want to spend more on adult education."

"It's not just our children who need education. As we said earlier, America keeps getting a wakeup call from the world," Lee continued. "You can't rest on outdated skills or outdated products. People are living longer; they will need to supplement their income and update their skills to keep job options open. It's not K-12; it's K-80. People say that you can't teach an old dog new tricks. As far as I'm concerned, you become an old dog when you *stop* doing new tricks!"

"Stop wagging your tail, John." Lynn bantered.

"You're right," John confessed. "I see it every day. You can't rest in outdated skills and expect to keep a job. Some careers that used to bring good salaries are no longer even necessary. If you don't keep learning, you fall behind very quickly."

"That's why conferences like the one we were at are so important," Lee continued. "As you know, my parents are all Swedish and grew up on the farm. They wanted my brother and I to experience what working on the farm was like."

"No late sleep-ins for you," Lynn said with a sigh.

"We were up before dawn to help milk the cows," Lee said. "We worked hard."

"Don't make it tougher than it was," Kelly said laughing. "They had milking machines. This story gets tougher every time he tells it."

"OK, we didn't have it too bad, but we did work hard," Lee confessed. "Hard enough to know that I didn't want to work on a farm all my life. And I was *motivated* to go to school so I wouldn't have to!"

"That's funny," Lynn said laughing. "And good thinking on the part of your parents."

"I also had the opportunity of meeting a very special great uncle, Uncle Harvey," Lee continued. "He had a way of collecting and sharing great quotes and quips he had stored away. He'd come up to us in the field and share wisdom."

"Wisdom?" John said smiling.

"He'd come up and say, 'I've got some wisdom for you.' My brother and I would roll our eyes but politely listen to this old man. He had a couple of quotes I remember to this day. He used to say, 'It's easiest to ride a horse in the direction it is going.' He'd just drop this line and leave. Now there is a whole seminar in that one quote. I mean, if you have a trend moving in a direction and you have the skills or the products to capitalize on it, you win big."

"Not a bad way to sell the importance of good strategic positioning," John confessed. "I'll have to remember that."

"His second horse quote was even better," Lee added. "He'd say, 'If the horse is dead, get off.' I love that. We all know people sitting on a dead career or an outdated product or service. They are whipping away, but that horse is going nowhere!"

"I love that," John continued to laugh.

"It's actually sad," Lee added. "Too many laborers are riding a dead horse and doing nothing to retool or reposition for the future. That's why adult education and junior colleges must be kept available and inexpensive so that everyone who is motivated to find their place in our future can do just that. I made up my own adage that I never got to share with Harvey. I love to say, 'Since it is hard to know if your horse is dying, have at least two horses.' In today's changing world, have a herd!"

"You are making too much sense to be a Republican," Lynn said.

"Look out now," Lee said with a smile. "I told you being Republican might be contagious."

"If we keep talking, they are going to make us help them sweep up the restaurant," Kelly said patiently, looking at Lee.

"I can see it now," Lee replied. "They found them at the table when they came to reopen."

"That isn't even funny, dear," Kelly said.

"Hey, we started early," Lee said. "Kelly and I wanted to have dessert at our place. We can carry on the conversation without taking up space here. That is, if you are still engaged enough to want to continue."

"I think we're game," John said, after looking to Lynn for a nod. "This has been one engaging conversation. Some of the other tables have been listening; do you have enough dessert for them?"

"Unfortunately, no," Lee said with a smile. "In fact, that brings us to the next area of focus that Republicans try to hold to—smaller government! Everybody wants a dessert, but they only want a few people to pay the bill."

"I want to hear this," John said. "I'm not sure even Republicans are that good at holding down costs."

"Now, you are hitting below the belt!" Lee said. "But that is worth looking at. We certainly don't always walk our talk either. I just think most politicians haven't got the guts to say no to *any* entitlement or government program. Once a program is started, they don't know how to stop it."

Waving to the waiter as he passed, Lee asked, "Could we have the bill?"

"Certainly," the waiter said smiling. "It will just be a minute."

"Don't worry about sharing dessert with more people," Lee said in a whisper to Lynn and John. "I don't want to share; I want leftovers. So eat light!"

"He's bad," Kelly said.

"You're guilty, too." Lee said. "In fact, that's the problem we have to face as a country. It's hard to resist all those special programs, but it isn't always better for our country or for those receiving those entitlements."

The waiter brought the bill and waited as Lee signed it.

"Thank you for a great meal and a great evening of service," Lee said.

"Yes, thank you," Lynn added.

"Just follow us," Kelly said. "Our home is only a few

miles away. We won't lose you. Lee never gets any willing Democrats to talk to. He will keep you in sight."

"You mean, if we tried to go home, he'd follow us?" Lynn said.

"I'm afraid so," Kelly sighed. "You're stuck with dessert and more conversation."

"It could be worse," John said with a smile as they got up to leave. "But we've only got a couple of more hours before we have to be on the road. Democrats obviously go to bed earlier than Republicans."

"We can wrap it up soon, I just want to make sure I tell you a couple of things that are really important to most Republican," Lee said. "I think you will agree when you hear them. I do promise to limit it. We do sleep, too."

"Do I have to sign a change of party registration to get permission to leave?" Lynn asked.

"Not required," Lee said laughing. "But Kelly does have the forms."

"You are bad!" Lynn said, shaking her head.

Chapter Nine

Shrinking Government Where You Can

"*I think you could probably merge agriculture and commerce and have one department of the economy. Instead, my prediction is coming true. I predicted in 1960 that, by the year 2000, there would be more employees of the Department of Agriculture than American farmers.... Cutting back on any government service is still anathema to liberals. Add to this the fact that in every developed country today, the strongest labor unions are government employees. In this country, they are probably two-thirds of our union members. So if you are a Democratic Party dependent on labor votes, cutting government services is not exactly popular.*" –Peter Drucker

★   ★   ★

"What a beautiful home!" Lynn said.
"Thank you," Kelly replied with a smile.

"Are there mountains out there?" John asked. "I can see lights."

"Those are hills, but we love them," Lee said humbly. "When we first came here, we could run up in those hills and run into herds of sheep. No room for sheep now."

"I'm sure it is still lovely," Lynn said.

"We're staying," Lee said. "It's our version of settling for smaller government. We're tired of moving for bigger, better, more expensive. We don't need bigger. We just helped our folks get everything down into a condo. No use making that tougher when we need to downsize. Besides it's the people we bring into a house that make it memorable."

"He's buttering us up again," John said laughing.

"Would you like some decaf coffee?" Kelly said.

"That would be wonderful," John said. Lynn and Lee nodded as well.

"What you said about smaller homes and smaller government sounds good," John said. "But I think you may have done a better job of doing that than some of the Republicans you have put in office."

"Since 1994, with Republicans leading the House and the Senate, we were able to keep

"What is necessary to make us a happy and prosperous people? A wise and frugal government, which shall restrain men from injuring one another, which shall leave them otherwise free to regulate their own pursuits of industry and improvement, and shall not take from the mouth of labor the bread it has earned. Were we directed from Washington when to sow, and when to reap, we should soon want bread. I own, I am not a friend to a very energetic government. It is always oppressive. If we can prevent the government from wasting the labors of the people, under the pretense of taking care of them, they must become happy." – Thomas Jefferson

spending under Clinton to an annual rate of just over 3 percent," Lee countered.

"Yes, but since Bush has been in, the federal spending has been racing out of control. The first three years under Bush, the government spending climbed by over 15 percent, and that number is adjusted to inflation. That puts Bush as the biggest-spending president since LBJ. How does he explain that to the Republican faithful?"

"Touché!" Lee said painfully. "I would have to agree; we have our own problems. Government spending keeps going up, but seldom as fast as it does when Democrats are in office. After all, Bush has had to deal with 9/11, two wars, and home-land security. It won't last. Holding the line for smaller government is probably the most common value Republican faithful talk about."

"I harp on this one all the time," Kelly joined in. "Lee even tries to calm me down. I have been writing Bush complaining! Government should be limited to the few critical roles that people can't do for themselves. That would mean keeping more money in the pockets of American citizens instead of funding another federal or state program. People are tired of the waste and fraud. They want to see an end to unnecessary programs, and they want them to avoid starting new ones."

"It's more than spending less," Lee said. "It's about who ought to be providing the services. Most Republicans feel that the power and resources should be kept close to the people through their local leaders rather than through a centralized and distant government."

"It's obviously easier talked about than done," John said.

"Look, the Bush budget calls for a real cap on the discretionary spending they can control. But I think there is more that needs to be done," Lee said. "We need to *throw focus instead of more money* at the problems we face. We need leaders who will foster a *scrounger mentality*. That means moving resources from the areas that are not making a critical difference to the areas that need those resources to do an even better job. We need to use a little more innovation instead of just asking for more funds!"

"It wouldn't hurt if we actually ended a few programs and departments," Kelly said. "Currently, too many programs actually have an incentive to fail. If they fail and keep failing, they just get more money and time to fix the problems that just keep growing. When the Department of Energy was established to coordinate an effective energy plan, we were importing 40% of our oil. We now import 60% of our oil. If that defines success, they deserve the increased funding they keep getting. After all, how did we manage to produce energy to fuel the world's richest economy before the department was created in 1977? There are now more people today working for the Department of Agriculture than there are American farmers; it's a crazy waste of your and our money."

"Some of those programs you want to cut serve real people," Lynn said. "They also hire real people in jobs they wouldn't have if you cut those programs."

"If those workers aren't making a real difference, they *should* lose their jobs," Lee said. "People in unnecessary jobs sap needed resources and talent. They need to retool and refocus their skills to find a job that does make a difference to something that is worth doing."

"That seems a bit heartless," Lynn said. "Some people have had those jobs for a long time."

"I'm not saying it's easy. I am saying it is important to do, or government just keeps growing. It's a basic issue we have to face," Lee continued. "Who needs to watch their budget in tough times—you or your government? Democrats never seem to want government to go on a diet. They are ready to raise taxes to support new and improved government answers to *every* American's problems."

"People talk about the *pain* involved in cutting government spending," Kelly said. "Painful for whom? Maybe it's painful for politicians in Sacramento and Washington, but as one of those average citizens who keeps paying the bills, I'd like to see a little less pain in our tax payment. No government in the history of the world has ever borne the cost of anything. It's the people who pay the cost!"

"Nice words," John said. "All politicians talk about cutting waste and unnecessary funding, but it isn't happening. If the Republicans in office could pass the cuts you want, what would that mean?"

"It starts with separating what we would 'like to do' from what we 'need to do,'" Lee asserted. "More and more citizens at the federal and state levels are depending upon services, programs and funding from the government. No one from either party wants the truly poor to go hungry or

"Every governor proposes moving boxes around to reorganize government. I don't want to move boxes around; I want to blow them up."
–Governor Arnold Schwarzenegger

for our country not to have an adequate military. But I think we ought to require a means-test for every citizen receiving state funds or government support."

"What would you cut that is unessential?" John said.

"What about money for the Endowment of the Arts and PBS?" Lee asked. "I'd cut funding in a moment if I could."

"That restricts artistic expression," Lynn said.

"As a citizen, I'd defend anyone's right to free expression. That is a guarantee of our Constitution, but the First Amendment does not guarantee a federal grant to fund that right," Lee said. "Let them compete for funding like everyone else. If people want to pay for art that trashes religion, they will make more of it. I just hate wasting public funds on it. Lower taxes and let people have enough money to enjoy the arts and support the ones that they value. We can make government smaller by funding only what is essential. The American government should not be in the arts business."

"I don't like a lot of that art either," John confessed. "But that is not a lot of money you are talking about."

"Every program and agency complains about needing more money or services will have to be cut," Lee said. "There is an alternative; fewer chiefs and more Indians. Corporate America long ago realized the importance of flatter organizations and fewer levels of bureaucracy. With enough Republicans in power, we could hold back funds from any program or agency whose administrative costs are out of line. Cut the appointments, the big salaries and the big offices. Require every department to have no more than five levels from the top to the bottom of the department. That would save big money."

"Agreed," John said. "With the Republicans in control of the White House, the Senate and Congress, how come these changes haven't happened?"

"Not all Republicans act and vote like Republicans," Kelly said. "I wish it were different. With filibusters and the political games that go on, you need more than a simple majority to get some of these changes through. We're hoping we can make this happen after this election."

"It looks like you might pick up a few seats," John confessed.

"I hope you two help that along next Tuesday," Kelly said.

"We'll see," John said.

"There is more that needs to be done to get costs under control," Lee added. "Require zero-based budgeting where every department and program must show value in order to earn funding for the next year. People in government like to say they have 'cut costs' when they have merely decreased the planned increase in funding. Some programs should be ended. Some should be scaled back. But every program should have to justify its investment instead of assuming they deserve last year's budget. Put a freeze on new programs unless mandated. When you can't afford the toys you have; don't buy new ones."

"I'm sorry to bring up Clinton," Kelly added.

"But you will," Lynn said laughing. "Republicans can't resist!"

"Every time President Clinton gave a State of the Union address I wanted them to show a required warning: 'This President is a noted 'Candy Man,' an admitted *misleader*. His promises are not to be trusted, and his programs if passed could be hazardous to *YOUR* wallet,'" Kelly continued. "Clinton once said to applauding Democrats, 'If you want to live like a Republican, you have to vote like a Democrat.' That says it all. The Democrats are the true *Party of Greed*—if you want to live off of successful Republicans, just keep the Democrats in power!"

> *"The deficit is like the guy that finds a rattlesnake in his pants. He knows he's got to shoot it, but he doesn't want to hit anything important."*
> *–Ross Perot*

"I think there is greed on both sides of the isle," Lynn said.

"I'm sure there is, but Democrats love to play Robin Hood," Kelly said. "They love taking from one group of Americans to give to another. Every time a Democratic politician speaks, I hear the cash registers sounding off as they rattle off new or expanded entitlements: Rebuild and modernize crumbling schools and reduce class size (Kaching!);...move toward universal health coverage, step by step, starting with all children (Kaching!);...double federal investment in medical research (Kaching!);...offer all our people lifelong learning (Kaching!);...provide high quality, universal preschools available to every child (Kaching!)!"

"It all adds up," Lee said. "I loved the late Senator Everett

Dirksen's great line: 'A billion here, a billion there, and pretty soon you are talking about real money.' It comes down to how parties define compassion. Remember, Democrats define compassion by how many people are 'helped' by government. Republicans tend to define compassion by how many people no longer need it. Democrats seem to say: 'I'm here to help you; you can't make it without me.' Republicans are more likely to say: 'I did it; this is how I did it; I know you can do it, too.'"

"Compassion comes in many forms," Lynn said.

"Our government bureaucracies are not known for their compassionate service," Lee said. "Let me take a question that Tony Snow, the Fox News commentator, loves to ask: When was the last time you went into the DMV and said to yourself, 'Can't you just feel the love here?'"

"Forced government compassion is not true compassion," Kelly said. "Give me freedom and the chance to respond to the needs of my fellow citizens. Faithful, decent American citizens are the most giving people in the world. When Americans are free to succeed, they are also free to rise to the occasion to provide a helping hand to fellow citizens when needed. Americans gave $1.6 billion in support of the victims of 9-11. That's compassion!"

> *"They that can give up essential liberty to obtain a little temporary safety, deserve neither liberty or safety."*
> *–Ben Franklin*

"That is impressive," Lynn said.

"America became great not because of what our government does but because of what our government does *not do*," Kelly said. "This country started out as a nation with limited governmental powers. I'm afraid we are in grave danger of losing that if it isn't already too late."

"Isn't that a bit extreme?" John replied.

"There is something that every American ought to keep on their wall," Lee added. "John Stossel has this great graph in his book, *Give Me a Break.* It shows Federal spending from 1789 to 2003. It's an amazing image of spending out of control! The line is all but flat until World War II. When America began, government cost the average citizen $20 in today's money. That's $20 a year! Taxes rose during wars, but for most of the history of America spending never exceeded a few hundred dollars per citizen. During World War II, government got much bigger. It was supposed to shrink again after the war. It never did; it just kept expanding. Now, the federal budget costs every man, woman and child in this country just above $10,000 a year. For you and me, it is obviously a lot more, but that is another story."

"That's a good perspective to see," John said. "But what people expect from their government has changed."

"Precisely," Lee countered. "And that is the problem. That change is not for the better as far as most Republicans are concerned."

"It isn't just the cost of government programs and agencies; it's the regulations and laws that limit our freedoms. You know the regulations and forms that your company has to fill out just to be in business," Kelly continued. "Too many rules and regulations are established to control the irresponsible few, but they end up swamping the majority of good and ethical businesses in paperwork no one reads."

"I understand," John confessed. "Some of the paperwork is unbelievable."

"It's one of the reasons corporations are leaving California," Lee added. "We win the prize for unnecessary paperwork."

"Agreed," John said.

"Regulations often hurt more than they help," Lee said. "Everyone talks about cleaner air and saving lives, but a study found that increases in fuel economy standards for cars in the early 1980s may have contributed to thousands of additional deaths, as automakers sharply reduced the size and weight of vehicles. Saving lives by passing more rules often has unintended consequences—more deaths somewhere else."

"The real world requires tough choices sometimes," Lynn said. "The environment and safety issues are not insignificant issues."

"Some laws and regulations are necessary," Lee added. "But every day you read about the silly rules out there that have replaced common sense. No nail clippers on flights. What is supposed to protect us ends up curtailing our freedoms. I mean, how can I fend off a terrorist on a plane without my nail clippers?"

"That's ridiculous," Lynn confessed.

"Democrats, and even some Republicans, seem to love unnecessarily controlling people," Lee added. "They want to control where and if you can smoke, how much water you can use to flush your toilets, where you can use your cell phone, whether and what kind of gun you can own, and, soon, whether you can drive an SUV without being labeled evil. I care about safety, but I value freedom even more. Our assault on saving people from themselves has resulted in some kids not getting to play dodge ball, playground areas being kept under lock and key, and people being encouraged to buy cars that may be more fuel-efficient but less safe."

"I'm glad there is no smoking in our offices," Lynn added.

"I am too, but it has gotten out of control," Kelly said with a smile. "I imagine that soon they will say that smoking is permitted in designated areas only. Today's designated area is Las Vegas, Nevada. In some cities, they won't even let people smoke outside. That goes too far, and it is the Democrats that usually take it too far."

"I remember a quote from a Russian manager I love to quote," Lee said. "Good old Vladimir Kabaidze, a Moscow entrepreneur, put it well, 'I can't stand this proliferation of paperwork. It's useless to fight the forms. You've got to kill the people producing them.'"

"That's terrible!" Lynn said laughing.

"Sign me up for the firing squad!" John said raising his hand.

"Now, they are having a few teamwork problems over there," Lee said. "But downsizing has gone quite well. All kidding aside, these regulations and the resulting bureaucracies tend to stifle the entrepreneurial spirit and the freedoms that are critical to our country's future."

"Republicans are into controlling as well," Lynn said. "They want everyone to think alike."

"It's the Democrats who are focused on controlling society through more laws and more regulations," Kelly said.

"George Bush is calling for a Constitutional Amendment to affirm marriage," Lynn said. "That isn't control?"

"Most Republicans want more freedom and fewer laws. Now, they *do want to promote* the cultural values and the self-control that makes the pursuit of life, liberty, happiness and the *American Dream* possible. Most Republicans feel that marriage and the preservation of the traditional family are both critical to the future of our society. I'm sure some would disagree, but I don't think that the Marriage Amendment is about being anti-gay. To many, it's about affirming the importance of a married father and mother in raising young boys and girls to take their place in the future. For centuries marriage has been defined as a union between a man and woman. Most Americans feel that shouldn't be changed."

"That's a form of control, isn't it?" Lynn asserted.

"Yes it is," Kelly continued. "But it has less to do with gays and more to do with what most people feel is best for children."

"Children?" John asked.

"I don't think people talk about it openly, but I think the Marriage Amendment is about what we will do with America's children. Even with their own statistics, less than ten percent of children will become gay. I think that number is even less, but that can be argued. The majority of children deserve to grow up in a home where they can experience both a mother and a father. If gay unions are given equal status to marriage, there will be no way that our society can legally make the choice to give a preference to heterosexual couples to adopt children who need a home."

"What about gay Americans and their children?" Lynn asked.

"There are good arguments for providing civil unions for gays, but they need not be called marriages," Lee said. "Many states have already moved to sanction gay civil unions. I think the number of states that will support such unions will continue to grow. I'm sure loving gay parents will keep their children. I just think society has a right to state that when it comes to adopting children, married couples should have a preference."

"I actually agree," John said.

"I do, too," Lynn added. "But I think gay civil unions should be allowed."

"No matter what the area, I'm sure we all agree that some controls are necessary, but some are more stifling than supportive," Kelly replied. "Democrats want more and more harassment laws and lawyers to impose them."

"I think there are excesses in imposing political correctness, but some Democratic controls make sense to me," Lynn continued. "I think environmental controls are worth regulating."

"Everyone is for responsible environmental protection, but the radical environmentalists want to do more than improve the environment," Lee countered. "They want to stop American capitalism. They don't like the profit motive, even though it's given us the most sophisticated pollution-control technology in the world. The Kyoto crowd wants to limit economic growth instead of freeing technology to address the problem. Not only can we creatively find ways to deal with environmental problems, the earth is a remarkable creation and is capable of great rejuvenation. We must take a long view. We shouldn't go out of our way to create problems, but neither should we buy into environmental hysteria that helps create donations to sustain environmental causes, but does little else. We have the right to use the earth to make our lives better, but we need to be responsible stewards of nature's gifts."

"The extremists do go too far," Lynn added. "What about gun control? You certainly support some gun control."

"I support more limits than Lee, but we have all the laws and limits we need now, if we would just hold people accountable," Kelly said. "You can't take atomic weapons out of the world because we don't like them. The atomic weapon card has been played and more countries now have it in the deck. To wish it away is impossible. Well, we will never get guns out of the world either. We just need to hold people accountable when they use guns in illegal ways."

"You support people being allowed to own guns?" Lynn continued.

"I do. In fact, when you look at the data, having the right to have concealed weapons decreases crime and weapon use in crimes," Kelly added. "In countries where guns are not allowed at all, only criminals have guns. As a result, what they call 'hot' robberies, that is robberies where people are robbed while in the home, dramatically increase. Criminals in those countries don't have to fear that citizens might have guns. Now, I sound like a NRA supporter, and I am.

> *"It's no accident that capitalism has brought with it progress, not merely in production but also in knowledge. Egoism and competition are, alas, stronger forces than public spirit and sense of duty."*
> *–Albert Einstein*

It's gotten to the point that they are vilified for all that is wrong every time a gun is used in a crime or mass murder. At the same time, I have no trouble with some limits."

"What limits?" Lynn asked.

"Actually, neither of us feel a need to justify citizens owning the semiautomatic and automatic weapons that are now out there," Lee added. "No one needs such a weapon for self-defense. In fact, it should be a crime to carry such weapons in public. That being said, criminals who are motivated will find weapons. So you have to be willing to convict criminals who use a weapon. Democrats seem to be more upset with law-abiding citizens having guns than criminals using guns."

"Both bother me," Lynn confessed.

"Do you have a gun?" Kelly asked. "We do."

"We do as well," John said. "We have it locked up, but we have one."

"That's really the point," Kelly said. "Citizens should have the right to use a gun responsibly."

"Let's get back to the central issue," Lee continued. "I don't know who said it, but it sure rings true for me, 'Government big enough to give us all we want is a government big enough to take from us all that we have.' Too many Americans are now dependent on money and benefits they receive from the government, while the productive, self-reliant, taxpaying public who make all these entitlements possible have become the *economically oppressed*. This isn't good for America."

"So government is bad," Lynn replied.

"No, we are blessed with a very special government in America. Government still has a role to play, but we must continue to keep the size of government smaller in comparison to our economy," Lee stressed. "Our job is not to eliminate government, but to focus our investment in government where it counts most. You can't love your nation and hate your government. There are too many great federal employees committed to making a difference. But we have to make sure we keep them doing just that. Republicans want leaders who will be fiscally tight where we can and a bit looser where government can make a difference that is important. Our goal is not to let any program get bigger than the value it provides. We need elected leaders who will declare war on waste, fraud and abuse. We will then have a lean but robust federal government."

"We need to support what works and trim what doesn't," Kelly said. "And then we all need to pay our fair share but no more!"

"Don't tell me," John said. "You also support Bush's tax cuts."

"I don't think he went far enough," Lee said. "But I support his effort to do what he could to stem the bleeding. We need to pressure Washington to make the tax cuts permanent."

"Want more coffee?" Kelly said smiling.

"I guess so," Lynn confessed. "Why don't you people just have us play cards like most couples do?"

"I love playing cards," Lee said. "But with an important election next week, I like taking care of America better!"

Chapter Ten

The Tax Man Cometh

"I don't think anyone objects to paying reasonable taxes and we all agree to the need to help the less fortunate. But, rich or poor, young or old, a person's reward for working more should always clearly exceed his reward for working less.... Americans aren't losing their confidence. They're losing their shirts."

–Ronald Reagan

★   ★   ★

"Since it's just you two, let me tell you what really upsets me about today's tax system," Lee said. "To me, having a fair tax system is a moral issue. Paying a fair tax ought to be *everyone's* responsibility! It's our country, and we all ought to pay to keep it going. You ought not to be able to disproportionately take from one group of Americans to take care of the needs of another group of Americans who are capable of taking care of themselves. Everyone but the poorest poor should pay a fair share of the nation's tax load. We are all blessed to be here in this great country. As we said before, most of *our* poor would be rich in many other countries. That's why I like a flat income tax—everyone pays the same percentage on every dollar earned. The rich and achievers of the world will always pay more, but at least everyone would pay the same percentage."

"Very predictable! I used to love watching *Crossfire*," John reacted. "Bob Novak used to say, 'The only reason God put Republicans on this earth is to cut taxes.'"

"I'm sure many would argue about whether God had anything to do with that, but there is some truth to his point," Lee confessed. "In fact, it's time for a little truth telling. Let me say what Bush is reluctant to say forcefully. YES, the lion's share of the tax relief of his tax relief plan has gone to the high-achieving, wealthy Americans because those same people *PAY* the lion's, donkey's and elephant's share of federal income taxes. American tax policy shouldn't be built on envy, but on equality."

"Whenever the Democrats are in power, they've been able to raise taxes," Kelly joined in. "Because they were able to persuade a large number of Americans that somebody else *should and will* pay the bill for the programs they want to create and fund.'"

"The wealthy can afford to pay more, and others can't," Lynn added.

"If that is the case, why should we limit progressive rates just to income taxes?" Lee asked. "Do you think the rich should pay more for food, movies, cars...I mean, why not have them pay more for everything they buy?"

"You're stretching it," Lynn said laughing. "No one is

> *"I strongly believe that anybody who votes should pay taxes. We keep taking millions of people off the income tax rolls. And if they don't pay anything, guess what, they don't care about how much government costs."*
> *–Stephen Moore*

suggesting that."

"No, the Democrats have just conditioned Americans to feel guilty for expecting fair taxes," Lee continued. "Common sense says we ought to have common taxes. If we each have the same vote, should we not pay the same tax rate? After all, if *one* *sales tax* is fair no matter what the income, why not one income tax rate?"

"The Democrats like to say it takes a village," Kelly added. "Well, let's have *everyone* in the village pay the same share so that *everyone* contributes to taking care of that village. What we have now reminds me of one of the tenants of Communism—'From each according to his abilities, to each according to his needs.'"

"Republicans love to look for communists behind every Democratic cause," John said laughing. "The viable communist regimes are now history, and the vast majority of Democrats are happy to see them go."

"OK, I'm not saying we are on the verge of becoming communist," Kelly admitted. "But in America today, wealthy taxpayers are held in involuntary servitude to every special interest that can slip its fingers into the public till. I just want to see an end to all this class warfare and bring sanity back to the tax system. Hearing Kerry and the Democrats bash Bush over and over on tax breaks for the rich drives me crazy."

"You think they are bashing Bush now? With the deficits we are facing, we can't afford the tax cuts Republicans have already been able to push through," John asserted. "And you want a flat tax? There would be screaming in the streets! That's no way to bring sanity back to the tax system."

"You have been listening to too many liberal spin-doctors," Lee countered. "I must confess that getting a flat tax is not on the immediate horizon. That has to be sold, and no one is selling. But America can't afford not to have the Bush tax cuts continued! No country ever taxes itself into an economic recovery, much less sustain its ongoing prosperity."

"That's what Reagan said," John continued. "And he drove us into a major deficit in the 80's."

"I'm so glad you said that because the Reagan years *did* produce a big deficit," Lee agreed.

"I can't believe you would admit that!" Lynn said smiling.

"The deficit was a fact," Lee explained. "But the deficit was not a result of the tax cuts; it was a result of the increased spending. Tax relief always stimulates the economy. Bush, Reagan, and even Kennedy knew that tax cuts are good for the economy *and* the federal coffers. A struggling economy needs a stimulant, not more government spending. Tax relief puts money to work in the economy which, in turn, produces more economic growth and more tax revenue for states and the federal government."

> *"The best means of strengthening demand is to reduce the burden on private income and the deterrents to private initiative imposed by our tax system; this administration has pledged itself to an across-the-board, top-to-bottom cut in personal and corporate income taxes."*
> *–John F. Kennedy*

"If that is true, why the deficit?" Lynn asked.

"Here's a little documented history," Lee answered. "Everyone was worried that when President Reagan worked to decrease the top marginal rates from a punishing 70 percent to 28 percent that the tax cut would break the budget in Washington. The result is clearly documented for anyone to read. According to the IRS, the federal tax revenue almost doubled from over $520 billion in 1980 to just over a trillion dollars in 1989. Unfortunately, the data also shows that spending in the 80's increased at an even faster rate than the revenue growth. It's the out-of-control spending that created the deficit; not the tax cuts!"

"I'm not sure that is the *whole* story," John countered.

"It isn't the whole story," Lee said. "It gets better!"

"I think you are losing it," John said sarcastically.

"No, the facts speak for themselves," Lee said. "During the Reagan years, the top one percent of *rich Americans* still paid more than 25 percent of all federal income tax while the bottom 60 percent paid only 11 percent. The poor were paying *20 percent less* of the income tax burden than before Reagan took office. The total *poverty population* decreased by nearly 3 million people and government spending on that group increased from $140 to almost $190 billion. Everyone talks about the success of the rich under Reagan. No one likes to give his policies the credit he deserved for improving the plight of the poor! Somebody once suggested that the charity of the poor is to wish the rich well. Instead of fostering class warfare, the Democrats ought to be a bit more appreciative. When the wealthy achievers do well, they invest what they make in companies that provide jobs, generate more tax revenue, and provide more examples of how the *American Dream* can still work. It is not wrong to want to better oneself and to enjoy the rewards of that success. It's what America is all about."

"Even if what you say about the Reagan years is true, it just seems like the Republicans are just throwing money at the rich who don't need it," Lynn said.

"The Republican approach is returning money to the Americans who pay the taxes," Lee said. "The American citizens who pay the bills deserve to receive relief proportional to what they paid in. Now, if some rich Democrats don't feel they pay enough, they can pay more and write a check to the government. The government will take it. I would rather donate to charities that will use my donation more responsibly."

"The tax relief for the wealthy that Bush has pushed through Washington is just too much," Lynn continued.

"My turn! I'm so glad you said that. The media loves to harp on Bush's 'big,' 'massive' and 'huge' tax cuts that are *un-*

fairly skewed in favor of the wealthy," Kelly said. "But they never share that the fact that the Bush plan offered a greater percentage tax reduction to lower- and middle-income families than he did for the wealthy. He also provided those reductions earlier. In fact, just like with Reagan, after implementing all of Bush's tax relief programs, the rich will pay *an even higher percentage* of the federal income taxes now than they did before his tax cuts went into effect. And more Americans will be paying *no income taxes at all!*"

"Is that true?" John asked.

"Yes, you can look at the numbers," Kelly said. "There are 44 million Americans who pay no income taxes or receive more money back than they pay in. That is 14 million more than when Bush came into office!"

"Look, it never occurs to Democrats that compassion may be due to the hard-working taxpayers who pay most of the bill," Lee added. "To the Democrats, there is no such thing as being mean to taxpayers. Besides, they think it's a matter of principle—tax money will always do more good in the hands of government than in the hands of the people who earned it."

"It's the working Americans who need the biggest breaks," Lynn said.

"Oh, you are doing a great job at hitting my hot buttons," Kelly added. "The Democrats want targeted tax cuts to the group of Americans that pay the least in taxes—their so-called *working Americans.* I hate that label. They are implying that successful high-achievers, small business owners and professionals who have studied and applied their skills to achieve the *American Dream* are not *working Americans*! I'm so glad Bush and the Republicans demanded a fair tax plan and put an end to this legitimized greed and tax redistribution."

"You haven't addressed the need of those working Americans," Lynn continued.

"I'm sorry," Kelly replied. "I just don't buy it. Every family in America has to deal with reality. They have to match what they spend with what they make. That means you have to have a budget and live within your means. Bush has made sure all tax-paying Americans have more money to spend. But the Democrats want more. Kerry and his Democratic colleagues want to take more from the wealthy so they can give more to the less for-tunate *working Americans* so they don't have to live within their means."

> "A government that robs Peter to pay Paul can always depend on the support of Paul."
> –George Bernard Shaw

"I wish I had the numbers like you have, but I've heard that in the tough times we have been through in the last few years that the wealthy have been the *only* Americans doing well," John shared. "They have just gotten richer."

"Not all have done well, but many are doing *quite* well. And I must confess that the success of most the wealthy has been good," Lee said. "Fair taxes encourage more people to put their wealth at risk to make even more. They won't risk their wealth unless there is an opportunity for even more reward. It's simple really. As Republicans, we try to help more people achieve the *American Dream* instead of punishing people who already have achieved it. Unfortunately, most Democrats work hard to create more dependence on programs and politicians in Sacramento and Washington instead of challenging people to learn marketable skills, start their own companies, work hard, save, invest and cap-ture their share of the *American Dream.* Fostering dependency and envy has never been the way to achieve success. It shouldn't be now. That's one of the major reasons I vote Republican."

"You really see it as punishing the successful?" John asked.

"Watching and listening to the Democratic Convention saddened me. They keep honoring Clinton and what he did for the economy," Lee said. "It was Clinton who legitimized envy and greed as founding principles of his tax policy."

"What are you talking about?" John asked.

"Clinton promised middle class tax relief in his 1992 campaign," Lee continued. "But once elected, none was given. Instead, in 1993, Clinton, with Gore casting the deciding vote on the deficit reduction bill, ushered in the largest tax increase in history not associated with a war time budget. Do you know who paid for that increase?"

"I was one of them." John said.

"Then you are fortunate, because 100% of that tax increase was paid by the wealthy," Lee said. "And since then, the Democrats' way of saying thank you for paying more of the freight on reducing the national debt, is to suggest that those people who had to pay more receive absolutely no tax relief and to redistribute what they paid in taxes to their favorite *working Americans.*"

"These have been a tough couple of years," Lynn asserted. "Many have lost their jobs."

> *"It must be remembered that the rich are people as well as the poor, that they have rights as well as others, that they have as clear and as sacred a right to their large property as others have to their's which is smaller, that oppression to them is as possible and as wicked as to others."*
> –John Adams

"They are not the only ones who are hurting. In the boom years, the Democrats loved pointing to the growing bounty for the rich from the booming stock advances and the great economy," Lee said. "But where were the Democrats when the stock market produced record losses, and the economic downturn forced many of the *rich* into bankruptcy. The hard-working achievers of the world have only one choice in today's crazy world—to support lobbyists and the political campaigns of those who will stand up to the liberal politicians and the media bias that supports them. Until Americans are willing to play by the same tax rules, that's the only choice they have."

"My mother taught me to say thank you," Kelly said. "What happened to gratitude in Washington? The Democrats deride these people instead of thanking them."

"It's more than that," Lee said. "If achievers are not secure in their enjoyment of property rights, no one is secure. If government can confiscate the wealth of a rich person, when will it take the income of the middle class? High taxes don't just hurt the rich; they hurt people who want to become rich."

"Paying taxes is a privilege," John said. "A painful one, but still a privilege."

"It certainly is, but that is a privilege that ought to be shared more equally with all who benefit from living in this great country," Lee said with a smile. "I'm proud to pay taxes, but I could be just as proud for a little less money."

"If it is such a privilege," Kelly said. "Maybe you ought to use the simplified income tax form the Democrats are trying to pass. The form says: 'How much money did you make last year? Send it in.'"

"Very funny!" Lynn said, joining in the frustrating laughter.

"The working Americans you complain about pay more than their share of the Social Security tax," John said. "Would you have a flat tax there as well so the rich would pay more?"

"No, I wouldn't," Lee said confidently. "The Social Security tax is not really a tax; it is more like a pension plan investment designed to insure some security for aging Americans."

"The rich still pay less," John confided.

"They will end up receiving less, because they have limits on what they can receive." Lee shared. "In fact, I have a feeling as the Social Security fund gets drained, I would bet you that there will be means testing before you receive any benefits from what you have put in. But that is another topic."

"I've seen this before," Lynn said. "I have a feeling we will hear more about this."

"Am I boring you?" Lee said.

"Boring you are not," Lynn replied. "I just get the feeling that all the questions I wish I had thought of will come to me tomorrow."

"Call me," Lee said with a smile. "I will be there for you. I'm loving this dialogue."

"I'm learning a lot," John said. "And you are making far too much sense for *my* own good."

Chapter Eleven

Change Social Security Now

"There are better ways to correct Social Security. One would be to start a new system for younger people, where a portion of the payroll tax that now goes to Washington to subsidize the national debt would instead go directly into the equivalent of individual savings or retirement accounts. Younger people would have more when they retired than they'll get with the current system, which, despite present surpluses, will go bankrupt sometime in the 21st century. The money would be invested in the real American economy, but the securities would belong to individual Americans. The numbers are potent. Take a 20-year-old today making $15,000 a year. If the payroll taxes (now $1,860, including the employer portion) were deposited each year into a retirement account earning the historic stock market average, he or she would have around $1 million at age 65." –Steve Forbes

★　★　★

"It's clear that the Republicans want to dismantle Social Security," John said. "My parents depend on it. They can't afford the deep cuts in benefits that changes will bring."

"You've been listening to those Democrats again," Kelly said. "We *evil* Republicans, who are supposed to have taken away benefits, have been in control of Congress since 1995. Who isn't getting her Social Security check anymore? Who is getting a smaller check? Well, nobody."

"They may be getting their checks, but the problem isn't going away," Lee said. "All you have to do to dismantle Social Security is to sit back and wait for it to dismantle itself in a generation. Social Security is a house of cards, and more people are moving into the house. Something has to be done. Those *deep cuts* you are talking about can be avoided if we allow workers to put some of their Social Security funds into voluntary, individually-controlled personal accounts. Future retirees may get less from the *traditional* benefit stream, but that would be more than offset by additional income from their personal accounts."

> *"In 1935, when the age for getting Social Security was set at 65, the average life expectancy was 59. If we adjusted for current life expectancy, the age of eligibility would be about 81 by now." —Martha Farnsworth Riche*

"Those personal accounts are invested funds," Lynn countered. "My folks also depend on Social Security. With the erratic performance of the markets after 9/11, I'm not so sure workers are as eager to invest those funds as they once were."

"That could be true," Lee agreed. "But stock investments held over 20 years or longer have always yielded positive growth. As the economy has come back, so has the market. They would have a choice; personal accounts wouldn't be mandated."

"The funds will not be safe," Lynn said.

"The last survey I read said that most Americans don't agree with you," Kelly said. "Even after the market problems and the Enron debacle, by a 2 to 1 margin surveys indicated that they supported giving younger workers the choice to invest a portion of their Social Security taxes in individual accounts similar to IRAs or 401K plans. The youngest working American workers supported such plans by a 4 to 1 margin."

"There is more to it than just winning a popularity contest," Lee added. "I'm sure you are aware that the infamous Social Security *trust fund* exists only on paper. It's not a savings account."

"In fact, while we are getting our facts right," Kelly said, "It was the Democrats under the leadership of Lyndon Johnson with his Democratic controlled House and Senate who took Social Security from being an independent fund and put it in the general fund so that Congress could spend the funds."

"People think there is a cave somewhere deep in Washington, DC with stacks of hundred-dollar bills waiting to be accessed when needed," Lee continued. "That isn't how it works. The U.S. Treasury receives *excess* Social Security tax revenue, and it immediately issues the *Social Security trust fund* an IOU. It then goes out and spends the money on retiring the national debt."

"That IOU is good," John said. "Blood would run in the streets if people found out that Treasury bonds were worthless."

"Of course, the IOU is good. It is backed by the full faith and credit of the federal government," Lee agreed. "It's good as long as the U.S. government is solvent and has enough money to pay the bills. But with us *Baby Boomers* coming, Social Security is going to have to change before all those IOUs are cashed in. Most Treasury obligations can easily be rolled over. When people cash in old T-bills and savings bonds, new ones are sold. But Social Security debt isn't so simple. As millions of us *Baby Boomers* head into retirement, their pension payments will have to be paid with actual dollars. Those are dollars the government doesn't have. No matter what kind of slight-of-hand politicians try to use, you cannot spend and save the same money. The government bonds the trust fund gets are not backed by tangible assets; there are no houses, factories, or cars we can repossess. They are just promises that can be kept by passing the problem to future generations. Future generations will have four choices: raise taxes on workers, decrease the benefits, increase borrowing or make the money we put into Social Security work harder for the workers. I mean, do you want to see a 50% tax increase on your children and their children?"

"Of course not," Lynn said.

"Then what do you suggest?" Kelly asked. "As the self-appointed *guardians of Social Security*, the Democrats love to scare seniors, but people are getting smarter. The attack ads and scare tactics are getting old, and I don't hear a lot of positive solutions coming out of John Kerry or the Democratic Party."

"I think the image of the future you are creating is the worst possible scenario," John said. "It is my understanding that Social Security's own trustees have suggested that, even if no changes are made, full benefits can be paid until 2038 with a slight drop of 30% after that."

"That's not a *slight* drop," Lee said. "Those are optimistic projections and seniors don't like even *slight* drops in benefits. Those will be *Boomer* seniors in 2038! This is no small problem. The Social Security system is not only heading for a train wreck; it is heading for a collision between two high-speeding trains you can't stop. People are living longer, and Americans are having fewer children. While it takes 3.3 workers today to support each retiree, by 2030 there will be only 2 workers for each retiree. That means more than a train wreck; it means intergenerational war!"

"I thought it was Alan Greenspan himself who headed the 1983 Social Security commission," John said.

"He did," Lee agreed.

"Under his leadership, they made a deliberate decision to build up a trust fund reserve to accommodate the *Baby Boom* bulge," John continued. "As a result when they get to 2018, they will have a $5 trillion surplus."

"That is a surplus based on IOUs," Lee reminded him. "Remember, no cash is being put in a cave. It just means that since 1983, Social Security has collected more in payroll taxes than it has paid out in benefits. If a real insurance company did to their premiums what our government has done with ours, their executives would find themselves behind the walls of your local federal prison."

"At its best, whether you look at it as a tax plan or savings plan, the return to workers in a traditional Social Security system is well under 2 percent," Kelly said. "Can you imagine the savings people would have if they invested that same amount, or even some of that amount, in personal accounts? I mean, we are not talking about day trading here. Only relatively safe investment options would be allowed. If they just put the money from their account in a Series I U.S. Savings Bond, they would earn over 3 percent."

"A hundred years ago the life expectancy of the average American was around 47 years. The gap between rich and poor Americans was considerable: about 10 years. It was not uncommon for a wealthy person to live into his late 60s or 70s, but quite rare for a poor man or woman to do so. Today the life expectancy in the United States is around 76 years, with the gap between the rich and poor a negligible 2-3 years."
—Dinesh D'Souza

"I like the idea of a cave," Lynn said smiling.

"Well, our politicians and our federal employees don't put their money in caves either," Lee continued. "Since 1984, they participate along with us in the Social Security system and are required to pay Social Security taxes, but they have an option we don't have. Many participate in what is called the Thrift Savings Plan. Depending upon when they started with the government and which pension plan they have, they have *the option* to contribute between 5 to 10% of their salary into tax-deferred stock and bond retirement funds. Some of those funds invest in stocks. All the fund choices are carefully approved by the government and are widely diversified to lower risks. They can play it safer and keep their funds in U.S. government bond funds, but they all do better than the current return on Social Security. It would be an improvement if they would just use their plan as a model for Social Security to give every American those options."

"I didn't know that they did that," John said.

"Few do, and they don't brag about their advantage. Let's get to the heart of this," Lee said. "What we are really doing here is trying to make sure we have a stronger security system for our children and grandchildren. If we do nothing, they will be the ones to pay the price."

"So you think the Republican plan will work?" John asked.

"I think the Republicans are smart enough to know that there is no one answer," Lee confessed. "But I do think they are putting out a positive vision that is connecting with the majority of Americans. Having a personal account, no matter what or how, will give people more control of their own future. That resonates with Americans. Let's protect the benefits of people who retire today, but let's strengthen and improve the system for future generations."

"You can't protect those benefits without raising the tax or decreasing the benefit," John continued.

"Then what makes you think we can do that in 2030 when there are more people in that situation?" Lee asked. "Little problems just become bigger problems when you avoid them. If we can meet that promise then, we certainly can meet it now. Bush has made that clear, his *Three No's of Social Security*—no benefit cuts, no tax hikes, no rise in retirement age. Under the President's guidelines for the Social Security Commission, the plan cannot reduce benefits or tamper with the eligibility age. A positive, pragmatic vision beats a negative, 'do nothing' vision every time."

"You think seniors will go for this?" Lynn asked. "Seniors vote."

"You bet they do! Nearly 30 percent of those who vote are over 60." Lee agreed. "All the Democrats used to have to do is whisper, 'They're taking your benefits away,' and it would send seniors into a frenzy. Not so anymore. I think more of today's seniors than most people do. These are some of the best and most caring citizens we have. When you give seniors the facts and you get them to focus on the future, they will support this. All you have to do is ask them if they have children. The hands will go up. You ask if they have grandchildren, and the hands will stay up. Then you ask, 'How many do not care about the retirement security of their children and grandchildren?' The hands will go down and their attention will be with you. They are smart, and they care."

"It would be nice to have low-income workers finally have a chance to accumulate some savings," Lynn confessed.

"With time, it would make everyone an investor and owner of part of what makes America work," Kelly added. "When people can't accumulate savings and wealth, they feel hopeless. We need to work together to give future generations hope. I realize that letting workers invest 2 percent of their payroll tax in one of three simple, pre-approved, privately-managed stock or bond portfolio funds would just be a start. I'd love them to stretch it to 5 percent, but that won't be easy to pass."

"Well, the Republicans have been in power and Bush promised to deal with this issue," John pushed. "If this is such a good idea, why have they not pushed to implement this?"

"Touching the nation's most politically volatile social program is tough enough," Lee said with a smile. "But after the 9/11 terrorist attack and the stock exchange retreat, it was pushed way back onto a back burner in the back of the White House kitchen. But I think it's time for a little more cooking."

"Some have suggested that they let different people put in different proportions into their accounts," Kelly said. "They would let lower income workers put up to 7% of their payroll taxes into personal accounts, and higher income Americans only 3%."

"You think that is fair?" Lynn asked.

"You know me well," Kelly replied. "Of course not, but I'm pragmatic. If this helps more Americans start to develop savings, I'm for it as a first step. More Democrats ought to be supporting this as well. With the fact that Social Security benefits are only available monthly means that those with shorter life expectancies, particularly black men, are treated far worse than those with longer life expectancies. Many die before they reach retirement age. They and their heirs get nothing for all they put in! That's just wrong! They would do much better under this plan."

"That is a problem," Lynn said, softening. "I'm glad to hear you say that."

"Social Security was never meant to be an investment vehicle. It was designed to provide income protection and a secure floor for financial security," John added. "Workers may not be able to pass a pile of saved money from Social Security funds on to their family, but they often forget the fact that almost a fifth of the benefits paid out are to survivors of deceased workers. They are getting some return."

"Yes, and that would continue. The personal accounts would just add to that," Kelly continued. "Look, Republicans care very much about all Americans. We just want more Americans to become successful. We don't like income redistribution.

I think this change in Social Security just might create the biggest anti-poverty program in America's history. And workers would be contributing to their own future every day. They'd be able to pass some of those savings on to their children when they die. Now, that ought to be a *big deal* for those *working American* Democrats love to talk about."

"One of these days, we might want to go all the way and learn from Chile which has been a model for retirement plans for their people," Lee said.

"Chile?" Lynn asked.

"In 1980, Chile led the way in providing average citizens with a decent retirement and strengthened their economy at the same time," Lee continued. "Prior to the 1970s, their people had virtually no savings. In 1981, their government-run pension system was replaced with a revolutionary, privately administered, national system of Pension Savings Accounts. After 21 years, their pensions were 50 to 100 percent higher than the pay-as-you-go plan would have provided. The cumulative assets managed by the funds are over 50% of their Gross Domestic Product. Their average return on investment has been over 10% per year. Similar plans have been created in Argentina, Peru and Columbia. Maybe some day, we'll be smart enough to do the same thing ourselves."

"The retirement age in all developed countries will have to go up to 75. Most people who reach 65 are perfectly capable of functioning. All present talk of financing Social Security is beside the point. The point is not money. The point is production."
–Peter Drucker

"I've read about their experiment. After the last few years, are they still doing well in those accounts?" John asked.

"The last information I saw was in 2002, and they were still going strong." Lee said. "They confessed that the plan was still in its teen years. It's not perfect, but their workers now have more choices and more people involved. But they expect the plan to reach maturity by the time the plan reaches 40. They will be ready to soar about the time ours comes crashing to the ground unless we listen and learn."

"I hope we do," Lynn said.

"There is another reason things are going to change," Lee added. "People are going to be working longer—not because they *have to*, but because they will *want to*. Companies are going to need them to work because we are not producing the number of workers we need to keep our economic growth going. The seniors we will have in the future will be healthier, more experienced and more open to working longer."

"More time to golf or more time to work?" John asked. "I'm not sure my choice is more time working."

"Not all will," Lee confessed. "But if more people are living to 100, I'm not sure how much golf people are going to want to play. I want to remain active and still take time to travel and enjoy life. And I think many like me will want to explore new models of employment that companies will have to create."

"What do you mean?" John asked.

"Boomers won't settle for working full time," Lee continued. "I think they would jump at a chance to supplement their income by working on projects for six months and then taking the rest of the year off. Smart companies will invest to keep their skills current, keep them focused on projects where their experience pays off, and pay them well to work where they are needed. If seniors have the added security of continuing to work with the ability to have better control of their retirement investments, people are going to be a lot happier about their future than they are now."

"What you are saying is new to me," Lynn said. "I just knew that Social Security was a problem. It seems like we have to act, but that there are things we can do."

"Then, I suggest you join our band of merry Republicans," Kelly said.

"You are persistent!" Lynn add. "And persuasive!"

"Persistent to the point of exhaustion!" Kelly added. "You folks must be tired of all this politics."

"One night a year seems an appropriate investment of time as an American facing an important election," John confessed. "But there are three areas you haven't touched on that everyone else is talking about—What can we and the world do to win the continuing war on terrorism, how do we handle the healthcare mess, and do you as Republicans think the Bush Guest Worker plan will help get a handle on the illegal immigration challenge?"

"Now, that's three full-day seminars for you!" Lee said. "Those are critical, tough issues."

"No, full-day seminars," Lynn said. "I refuse to move in with Republicans! I mean, what would my liberal friends say?"

"OK, we'll give you a quick and dirty look at all three before we end this merry medley of momentous monologues and get to go to sleep!" Lee said with a smile.

"Pardon my husband," Kelly added. "He's losing it."

"No, I'm not," Lee countered. "Let's get the easy one over with first. When America faces an enemy, the vast majority of Americans want Republicans in control. That is one reason Kerry will lose to Bush on Tuesday."

"I'm glad you think that is easy," Lynn said. "*This* minority sitting in *this* seat is not yet convinced."

Chapter Twelve

Maintaining Military Strength and Homeland Security

*"In war: resolution. In defeat: defiance.
In victory: magnanimity. In peace: goodwill."*
—Winston Churchill

★   ★   ★

"It ought to be clear by now that the war on terrorism is not going away," Lee said. "There is no one country to defeat. They have learned to hide in civilian areas around the world in cells that are hard to find, much less infiltrate to get security information. You aren't just beating terrorist enemies; you must compete for the hearts and minds of people who are training future terrorists."

"I'm afraid it's not going away, because Bush wasted time and world support on fighting an unnecessary war in Iraq," John interrupted.

"I don't agree," Lee said. "Everyone agreed Iraq had weapons. They only disagreed on whether war was the appropriate response. The jury is still out on whether they had weapons of mass destruction and what they did with those they had. But you have to agree that the landscape of the Middle

131

East has radically changed and a cruel tyrant has been taken from power. Iraq has not yet been transformed into the free republic we want it to be, but it is far ahead of where it was. Syria and Iran are isolated. Democracy and dreams are starting to blossom. It will take time, but it is happening and surveys show that the majority of Iraqi citizens appreciate it."

"Not all," Lynn said.

"Not all? When a President gets 53% of an election, it's a landside!" Lee said with feeling. "We will never have everyone agree here, much less Iraq. The biggest problem with Iraq is that those who disagree fire guns and plant bombs. They also have invited their terrorist friends from the neighborhood to join them. Our troops and our diplomats have targets on their backs. There is no question that it is still dangerous there, but more and more parts of Iraq are living more normal lives."

"More people have lost their lives after Bush said the hostilities were over than we lost in winning the war," John said.

"That's true," Lee said. "I told Kelly at the time that winning the war was too easy. Their army wasn't defeated; it just quit and went into the civilian masses. Some have been getting even ever since. But still, the silent Iraqi majority says in the polls that they are glad we came here, but to say so publicly in Iraq is to risk being killed."

"My mind goes back to history: How many lives might have been saved if appeasement had given way to force earlier on in the late '30s or earliest '40s? How many Jews might have been spared the gas chambers, or how many Polish might be alive today? I look at today's crisis as 'good' vs. 'evil'—Yes, it is that clear. Sometimes in life you have to act as you think best— you can't compromise, you can't give in—even if your critics are loud and numerous."
–George W. Bush

"The war isn't done," Lynn said.

"I couldn't agree more," Lee replied. "Real wars have bad days where you even lose ground. It isn't a movie where every hero lives. This is more like a soap opera. Our job is to keep this serial mostly positive on our journey to true freedom in Iraq. And it won't be done any time soon, but we now have an outpost for emerging democracy and a buffer for terrorism that is impacting Iran, Syria and Saudi Arabia. That's why terrorists are fighting so hard to get us to leave. In fact, our being there is empowering good people in all those countries to call for more freedom and opportunity. We aren't losing; we are gaining big time. The liberal media just focuses on the problems. The problems are real, but they are not covering the real story—the thousands of personal stories of success. All the negative news is doing what the terrorists want; it's attempting to undermine the support of the American people for the war and for President Bush."

"I remember when Secretary Rumsfeld said he wasn't even confident we can win this war!" Lynn said.

"He's a rock-solid realist," Lee said. "Overconfidence is not one of his faults, but he remains optimistic. In fact, thank goodness we have an optimistic defense secretary. As I said earlier, optimism isn't Pollyanna Thinking; it is based on the belief that

> **"To be prepared for war is one of the most effective means of preserving peace."**
> **–George Washington**

in realistically looking at the obstacles we face, we can find a way to overcome them. He knows we need to change how the military is structured to meet today's enemy. He's consistently working to do just that, and he won't stop until he gets some needed changes."

"Even though I am not a big fan of using the military, I actually like Rumsfeld," Lynn said cautiously. "I love it when he tells it like it is. Most of the time, I don't agree with him, but he is not afraid to speak his mind. Not enough in Washington do."

"I like his style," John agreed. "But I don't like a lot of his decisions."

"In a world with more rogue countries and terrorist groups capable of attacking our homeland and vital global interests, America has to be strong. To defend its freedom and way of life, we have to invest adequate resources in the military to remain strong, flexible and technologically sophisticated. Today, we use air power as a precise and overwhelming attack force; we add a good dose of special forces and on-the-ground intelligence. The rest of the military force must be defined not by mass and numbers but by mobility and swiftness," Lee continued. "You may not like fighting our wars where the terrorists live, but, like Bush and Rumsfled, I'd rather fight terrorism on their ground than ours! No matter what the changes or the challenges, both men have the resolve to win this war. I'm willing to match that."

"Why not use the U.N. as Kerry suggests?" John said. "We missed an opportunity to build a strong international coalition with U.N. support."

"Bush listened to Colin Powell and went the extra mile, and we ended up wasting time trying to do so!" Kelly said. "Don't get me started on the U.N.; it has *never* been able to be an effective military force. It's like winning a war by committee. They don't act; they just talk, disagree and put off action. Bush would have been better to build a quick coalition of the willing, democratic nations and use that as a base for action. I'd call it U.F.A., the United Freedom Alliance. The only way you could join it is to be a democratic country committed to the rule of law, free enterprise, and freedom. In fact, I'd limit most of our foreign aid to such countries; there should be rewards for standing for freedom and free enterprise. But this is a whole other issue, and I made Lee promise to limit himself to three topics. And now Lee is giving me one of those looks that *I'm* the one breaking the rules here."

"Looks aside; that's interesting," John said thoughtfully.

"The U.N. has its flaws, but it should not be ended."

"I didn't say to end it," Kelly said. "It's still a place where all the world's countries can come to talk and deal with diplomatic issues. It also can be a force for humanitarian good that unites all countries in dealing with global catastrophes, but it is not going to be the source for a viable military force. I certainly wouldn't support it with the funds we give it now. It's not worth what we pay to have others use the funds to do what we don't want done. But let's forget this thread. The U.N. is now involved in a limited way in Iraq, and that's good. The U.N. is just not the answer to the world's terrorism problem."

"What is?" Lynn asked.

"America and its coalition of allies are the best answer we have. They must stay focused, and they must have the resolve to see this through," Lee confessed. "It's not real complicated. It's Teddy Roosevelt all over again, 'Walk softly and carry a big stick.' We have the biggest, most technologically sophisticated stick in the history of the world. But we also have a heart of compassion that wants our enemies to give up and get on with letting us help them rebuild. We want peace, but we are strong enough to use force when needed. We need firepower and brainpower, strong allies and effective diplomacy, along with courage and patience. When I see those bumper stickers that read, 'War is not the answer,' I want to cross out 'not' and write in 'sometimes.' War is *sometimes* the answer. We shouldn't seek it out, but we shouldn't shrink from it either."

"In a way, I agree," John said. "We must be strong. I just think we have gone overboard in Iraq."

"We must go overboard to deal with an enemy that is committed to kill thousands and is hard to find," Lee said. "We must never forget to learn from our past leaders. At the Constitutional Convention when our founding fathers were forming our great country, they proposed limiting the U.S. standing army to 5,000 men. George Washington responded by requesting a clause that would limit the size of the invading army to 3,000 troops. The laughter that followed resulted in them dropping the proposal. I sure wish we could limit the investment we make in our military, but the world does not guarantee that our enemy will abide by the limits we want to impose on them. We must stay *very* strong."

"That's funny," John said. "There is also a lot of truth in what you *and* George Washington have said. But you can't say that Washington was a Republican!"

"With statements like that, he would have been," Lee countered.

"No way of knowing," John said with a knowing smile. "We certainly need to be strong, but a lot of the Department of Defense budget can't even be accounted for."

"That's true," Lee replied. "That concerns me as well. They need to be accountable for how they spend their money. As Rumsfeld has been trying to do, we have to change how we invest our funds and our people so that we deal with today's threat. The World War II General and diplomat George C. Marshall used to say, 'The generals like to fight yesterday's wars.' We have to make sure we are not falling victim to that same tendency. We won't have won the war of changing the military until we take funds away from the outdated side of the military and invest it where it can make a difference in today's wars."

"I'm surprised to hear you say that," Lynn said.

"I want security," Lee said. "As Rumsfeld loves to say, 'Weakness is provocative.' But I don't want to give the military a blank check. Remember, Republicans want as small a government as we can get, but staying ahead of our enemies is expensive. Former Defense Secretary Cap Wienberger used to say, 'You don't just go out to the store and buy high-tech weapons on the day you need them.' We have to stay ahead."

"I'm still afraid that the war in Iraq has turned into a holy war," Lynn continued.

"This isn't a war against Islam," Lee said. "Most Moslems aren't even living in the Middle East. But some of the most militant do. In the Middle East, Islam has been hijacked. And it isn't by just a few hijackers. When 50 % of those hijacked seem to be applauding for the terrorists, we have a *big* problem. Even worse, the other 50% aren't exactly clamoring to join the fight to retake the plane."

"It reminds me of what Israel has to deal with every day," Kelly said. "I remember reading that death reports for Palestinian suicide bombers are listed as wedding announcements. They list the name of the terrorist who died in the bombing and announce his 'wedding with the black-eyed beauties for eternity.'"

"Is that true?" Lynn asked.

"Yes," Kelly said. "But you don't have to look far to find similar examples of how Palestinians, and now some Iraqis, celebrate the death of Israeli and American soldiers."

"That's the problem," Lynn continued. "It just perpetuates the cycle of violence that is…"

"'Cycle of violence' is an inappropriate description with Israel, much less the United States," Lee interrupted. "There is no cycle of violence. One side has religious fanatics who are violent, hateful and committed to taking out their hatred on innocent civilians with the support of radical religious leaders and a state-controlled press. The other side rejects indiscriminate use of military force, and their free press and religious leaders complain when there are civilian deaths and excesses result."

"That's naive," Lynn countered.

"It's naive to think otherwise," Lee said. "Israel and the U.S. respond when attacked in defense of liberty. They use their military to respond to terrorism, not foster it. One side teaches their children to sing songs of peace but to remain strong. The other side teaches its children songs of blood, fire and hate.

Civilian attacks occur and the majority of Arab leaders remain silent while the Arab streets participate in militant outrage. Why is Israel in the West bank? Because they where attacked in the 1967 war and won. At the same time, Israel has proven that it can give land for peace and get along with Arab neighbors. They have proved that with Egypt and Jordan. If the Palestinians would give up on their mission to drive Israel from the Middle East and rise up against the terrorist attacks they now support, peace would be possible. There would be no 'cycle of violence,' if the terrorism would stop!"

"Not all are supportive of the terrorists," John continued.

"That is true," Lee said. "Not all Moslems are terrorists, but all the terrorists who attacked us on 9/11 were Moslem!"

"It doesn't warrant killing thousands of innocent civilians in Afghanistan and Iraq!" Lynn said with feeling.

"I'm sure we would all agree that most Americans, Democrats and Republicans alike, want to limit civilian deaths. We invest heavily in creating weapons to limit collateral, civilian damage," Kelly said. "But let's be honest about what we are dealing with here. You want to see civilian casualties? Look at World War II in Germany and Japan. In recent wars, the estimates on civilian casualties are notoriously overstated early. At first, they said 4,000 Afghan's died in the recent war, but

"In the final analysis, America and her partners will be measured not by how we wage war but how we make peace.... We will have before us an historic opportunity. From the confluence of the Tigris and the Euphrates, where civilization began, civilized behavior can begin anew."
–George H. Bush

later more exacting estimates by the *LA Times* and Reuters settled for just over a thousand. They overestimated civilian casualties in the first Gulf War; they claimed nearly 20,000 early. Accepted estimates after the war were under 3,000. The terrorists know we value civilian life. That is why they hide behind them. They make it tough, but our military works overtime to protect innocent civilians. They do a great job in doing so; sometimes it costs them their lives."

"I don't want to get bogged down in the Iraqi war!" Lee said. "The issues are bigger than that, and they go beyond how well we fight. We must win the war of peace."

"Are we?" Lynn asked.

"I think we are. We need to continue to invest in the future of the *new* Middle East. We now have launched Radio Sawa and Al-Hurra TV, our version of 'Radio Free Iraq,' to win their hearts and minds through our words, our actions and the freedom and opportunity we support. But I still don't think we are doing enough at winning the peace. We won the war of peace with Japan and Germany. We must have the will to win the war for peace in the Middle East. If they would only get the message of history—There's nothing better than to lose a war to America! We always try to fix what we break."

"I agree with that," John said.

"Then maybe you can write John Kerry and some of your Democratic politicians and encourage them to give the administration the funds and support they need to do that," Lee said with a smile.

"I could do that," John countered. "It would be easier for me to do that than vote Republican."

"You mean, I haven't changed your mind yet?" John said.

"You're certainly bending it," John confessed.

"I'm more of a pacifist that John is," Lynn said cautiously.

"I believe people have the right personally to choose not to defend themselves," Lee said. "But I don't think they have a right to demand that others commit suicide by proxy. When you don't punish evil, you encourage it."

"Nonviolence has worked before," Lynn said.

"It has worked because those who promote it are a vocal minority," Lee said. "They get the press coverage to turn the hearts and minds of moral people who are prone to compassion. But those same demonstrators let other people fight their wars and save the freedom that gives them the right to demonstrate."

"That's pretty cynical," Lynn said. "What about Gandhi and Martin Luther King, Jr.?"

"The work of Gandhi against British imperialism in India and Martin Luther King's stand against American racism were major moral achievements in world history," Lee said with feeling. "Nonviolence was an appropriate effective and moral response, because British and American leaders were subject to moral and legal restraint in a moral country loyal to the rule of law. Against Stalin, Hitler, Pol Pot, Idi Amin, Saddam Hussein, and Osama bin Laden, nonviolence would be suicidal and ensure the victory of evil."

"You cast a pretty wide blanket for evil to stand on," Lynn said.

"I just shudder to think what would have happened to the Western world had Churchill taken the advice of Gandhi when he wrote an open letter in 1942 to the British People," Lee said.

"I didn't know he did," Lynn confessed.

"His message was printed in the British press, and, thankfully, his plea was denied, even ridiculed," Lee said.

"What did he say?" Lynn asked.

"I've got it here in this book," Lee said searching for the dog-eared page. "Gandhi wrote: 'I would like you (the British) to lay down the arms you have as being useless for saving you or humanity. You will invite Herr Hitler and Signor Mussolini to take what they want of the countries you call your possessions....' He later adds, 'If these gentlemen choose to occupy your homes, you will vacate them. If they do not give you free passage out, you will allow yourselves, man, woman and child to be slaughtered, but you will refuse to owe allegiance to them.' Thank God that England had Churchill instead."

"That does seem extreme," Lynn agreed. "But Churchill wasn't fighting Germany for the oil companies that supported his campaign."

"You have been listening to too many Democratic talking points," Kelly said. "I would feel the same way if what you said was true."

"How do you know it's not true?" Lynn said assertively. "I don't receive *any* talking points. I am concerned about the Republican ties to oil interests."

"I am sure that keeping the oil supplies available is one of the strategic reasons we care about the Middle East," Kelly said. "But the United States bends over backwards not to abuse its position. We acted with our allies to free Kuwait from Iraq in the Gulf War. If anyone had a right to demand exclusive oil contracts, we did. Do you know what percentage of oil from Kuwait comes to the United States?"

"I don't know," Lynn said. "I'd assume a good percentage would be controlled by our oil companies."

"Three percent," Kelly said. "Three percent! Kuwait

"A number of times...foreign tyrants, warlords and totalitarian dictators have misinterpreted the well-known likeability, patience and generosity of the American people as signs of weakness or even decadence... But...when the emotions of the American people are aroused, when their patriotism and their anger are triggered, there are no limits to their national valor nor their consuming passion to protect this nation's cherished tradition of freedom.... (American) history is littered with the wreckage of regimes who made the mistake of underestimating the vigor and will of the American people."
—Ronald Reagan

alone could have sold us all the oil we need to import, and it likely would have been glad to. But we didn't. We gave the country and its oil fields back to its government. We let them get the best deal they could get on the free market."

"That is hard to believe," Lynn said.

"Check it out," Kelly said. "While you are at it, make sure you look into existing Iraqi oil contracts prior to our military campaign. It was France and Russia who had long-term economic and oil contracts with Iraq. They had the strongest oil interests in thwarting any U.N. action in Iraq. Time will tell, but early indications are that America is working hard to insure that Iraq's oil reserves are used to rebuild the country, not line our oil companies' profits."

"War still concerns me," Lynn said.

"Remember what I said?" Lee asked. "War is *sometimes* the answer. It was war that destroyed Adolph Hitler, not talk or negotiations. In fact, I've heard it said that no country in history has ever shed more blood for the freedom of others than the United States. There were no oil interests in Germany, in Korea, in Vietnam and in Kosovo. We support Taiwan; there's no oil there. We have been willing to take stands in support of freedom. Freedom has never been free."

"It shouldn't happen often," Lynn said.

"I agree, but the war issue is irrelevant now. We need to win the battle for peace whether you were for or against the initial campaign. Democrats and Republicans alike ought to be doing what they can to support our troops and the emerging Iraqi government. It would be wise for everyone to remember the words of Abraham Lincoln in his Gettysburg Address," Lee said. "Where he honored the soldiers who had died for our country: '…We here highly resolve that these dead shall not have died in vain— that this nation, under God, shall have a new birth of freedom— and that government of the people, by the people, for the people, shall not perish from the earth.'"

"You've memorized that?" Lynn asked.

"Yes," Lee replied. "That short address said so much about what America is about."

"I hope none of us ever forget the price our soldiers have paid," John said.

"I'm glad to see that the memorial to World War II veterans is taking its place on the Washington Mall," Lee continued. "We are finally waking up to some aging heroes that humbly participated in the turning point of a century. The books and movies about our graying veterans in their best hours have been inspiring a nation not known for its appreciation of military history. I just pray that those who are alive get to see the new National World War II Memorial. How should we honor such men? I think the best way is to not forget their legacy and to promise to be prepared and armed in a way that no generation will have to repeat what they went through."

"You sound like Bush," Lynn said.

"I told you. When it comes to the military, Americans trust Republicans," Kelly said. "A strong military and homeland security remain big issues, and it will always remain a big issue. Evil still exists. It must be opposed. Evil also has a way of finding its way into the hearts and minds of new enemies, and the toys evil plays with are getting worse and worse. We can't rest in past victories."

"I like what P. J. O'Rourke said when he spoke at the Reagan Presidential Library a couple years back," Lee said with a smile. "He said, 'Republicans are the *squares*. They actually know how to use guns. The liberals would still be fumbling to get the trigger locks off the guns.'"

"That is bad," Lynn said.

"He's right," John said, joining in the laughter.

"Look, I told you that this was an easy issue to sell," Lee replied. "Even if good people disagree about whether or not we should have gone into Iraq, we have gone in. You can't go back and undo it. The best strategy is always to get busy investing any time we might waste on blaming and whining into making the best out of what opportunities lay ahead. We cannot afford to lose this war. We either fight terrorism there, or we will end up fighting them on our streets. The strength of America was forged not out of easy times, but out of great men and women who had the fortitude and the drive to overcome whatever obstacles were in their way. We have to keep that resolve to meet today's enemies. I think President Bush has shown that resolve. That is why I believe that America will give him another term. Kerry shows no such resolve."

"He will get that second term," Kelly said with a smile.

"With warriors like you two on his team, I don't doubt it," John said shaking his head.

"I think that was a compliment," Lee said.

"It was," John answered. "I wish I had the same zeal for my party and our candidates. The more we talk, the more I realize I don't."

"Neither do I," Lynn said. "But Republicans can always look good supporting war. What are you going to do to deal with immigration and healthcare? Those are tough issues for both parties."

"Did you notice how I left the tough issues for the last?" Lee asked.

"Yes," Lynn said smiling.

"I was hoping you would be falling asleep," Lee continued. "But it doesn't look like that is going to happen."

Chapter Thirteen

Healthcare Is Sick and Getting Sicker

> *"Instead of paying a large (health insurance) premium every month for services you may not use, I believe we ought to have an account that allows a person to pay a much smaller premium for major medical coverage, and then put the savings into a health account, tax free. The money is your money...not the government's money. If you don't use it, it's yours to keep. And for the more affordable premium, you also get catastrophic care, protection in case of serious illness."*
> *–George W. Bush*

★ ★ ★

"The Democrats have a plan for healthcare," John said. "Where is the Republican plan?"

"The Democrats have floated numerous plans! As usual, Kerry is promising access to high-quality, affordable healthcare to every American," Lee agreed. "But they want to increase taxes or role back tax relief to pay for it. Their proposals also bring us closer to a national, government-controlled healthcare plan that we rejected when Clinton tried to push it through."

"Times are different," John said. "People may be ready now."

"I'm not. The plans they have floated are complicated or just more of the same with the taxpayers just having to pay a bigger bill. Some of the Democratic candidates even proposed a Constitutional Amendment establishing healthcare as a right. Look, there is one thing I definitely do not want," Lee said. "I don't want what they have in Canada or the UK. There are long waiting times for seeing medical specialists and a growing black market for care. In Canada, over 25% of patients wait more than 4 months; in the UK, it is nearly 40%. In Saskatchewan, the birthplace of Canada's government health care, median wait times for surgery increased from nearly 10 weeks in 1993 to 29 weeks in 2001. Sometimes that kind of wait can be fatal. A single-payer system promotes higher taxes, limits technology and drugs, produces waiting lists, rations care, and prolongs suffering. I don't want that kind of care here. That is not progress."

"Having to wait is not one of my greatest joys either, but life expectancy in Canada is higher than it is here in the states," John asserted. "They must be doing something right."

"That may be true," Lee agreed. "Healthcare is not the only factor in life expectancy. Americans are twice as likely to be obese than Canadians, and we have a higher murder rate. I don't think any of us are proud of those facts, but it's important to stay focused on the healthcare choices that *we* face."

"Theirs is a very different system. Waiting in line to be seen is not the only waiting Canadians have to put up with," Kelly said. "They wait for new medicines to be developed and approved. They may get medications for less, but they have fewer medicines to work with. Their policies dry up costly research in their own pharmaceuticals. They leave the major challenge of developing new drugs to the U.S. and then want those drugs for less."

"They get them for less," John replied. "And so do many Americans who buy their drugs through Canadian suppliers."

"Of course," Kelly said. "Everyone wants drugs for less, but all the politicians and citizens want are lower prices. That has little to do with lowering the costs to the pharmaceutical companies. It costs hundreds of millions of dollars to develop new drugs. It also takes a lot of resources to train even a single new doctor. There is no free lunch for medical advances and competent physicians, even though politicians get elected by promising free lunches. No matter what kind of shell game you play to shift the costs, those costs don't go away."

> *"Hell-bent for universal insurance, we should be hell-bent for universal high-quality health care. By no means the same; they often conflict. Insurance provokes unrestrained spending; spending provokes rationing. The plastic health card won't treat anybody. Doctors do."*
> *–George Ross Fisher, MD*

"They don't sell those drugs at a loss in Canada," John said. "The pharmaceuticals are making a profit. They just don't make the profit they get from soaking us here in the states."

"The Canadian government has the advantage of ordering drugs for an entire healthcare system," Lee confessed. "They have a take-it-or-leave-it control over the pharmaceuticals who do not want to lose market share even when their profits are cut. The Canadian government doesn't really set the price; they let the pharmaceuticals set the price, but only within set guidelines. The firms know that if they don't give a price within those guidelines legal action can result. They can't exceed the highest Canadian price for existing drugs treating the same disease. If it is a breakthrough drug, they must charge no more than the median price for the same drug price established from seven other key countries and their prices. They also can't increase prices beyond the general rate of inflation in Canada. This cuts the profit. Now, for pharmaceuticals to put capital at risk to create new drugs, they have to make a profit large enough to make that risk profitable. Since they don't get that profit in Canada or the UK, where do you think they are forced to get that profit?"

"In the U. S. of A.," Lynn said with a wry smile.

"That's right, and we should be upset," Lee continued. "We are paying the higher price to cover the higher costs of creating new drugs and new medical technology. It isn't fair, but I'm not sure anyone has an idea on how to stop it."

"You're admitting you don't have all the answers?" Lynn asked, smiling again.

"My wife lets me know that every day," Lee said laughing. "I do know what doesn't work. Price controls done in every country would just mean more needless suffering and premature deaths as the supply of new drugs and new technology dries up. It also needs to be said that even though the Canadians get our drugs and innovations for less, remember, they don't have access to as many of those drugs and equipment. Even when the national government approves a new drug, the provinces are not required to offer it. It can take years for a new drug to make it into a provincial hospital's list of drugs doctors can prescribe. We also have almost twice as many MRI machines per patient."

"Maybe we have to face the fact that we can't afford all these innovations and medical gadgets?" John asked.

"Not so fast; America is rich," Lee said. "We can afford the best system in the world. Right now, 14% of our economy is spent on healthcare. In the early 1970s, that figure was 8%, which is what the UK spends now. Canada spends 9% and Germany 11%. But what do we get with that extra investment? We get more drugs, more technology, and more options for care. Even though we can afford it, I'd rather get more for the money we spend! The trick is to spend that investment more effectively and give individual citizens more choices, better quality and more control. I think we can get a far more efficient and quality system by making some key changes."

"The poor won't be able to afford those choices you talk about. For far too many, people are forced to choose between food and medical treatment," Lynn added. "It's just tragic. That's why we need a universal healthcare system."

"Even if people are currently being forced to choose between food and medical treatment," Lee countered. "It would be better to make sure we set aside the money needed to take care of the poor than to impose a government-controlled program that traps us all in a system that won't work."

"OK, what do you suggest?" John asked.

"If I were *King*," Lee said, pausing.

"A *Republican King*?" Lynn added.

"Of course, it would have to be a *Republican King*," Lee said. "Now, I know it's not possible, but if I were, I would first have to admit that changing our healthcare system is like trying to fix a very big, racing engine while the motor is still running! There are no easy fixes, and I acknowledge that. With those excuses said, let me confess that incremental changes won't fix it. But many are floating ideas that I think could work."

"Honey, with the frustration and anger out there, we may not *need* a king to make this happen," Kelly said. "I think John is right. Things are getting bad enough that people are going to *demand* a change. People are stuck in jobs they hate because they can't afford the COBRA policies they would be stuck with if they left. Too many ended up with times when they had no coverage at all, and they now face underwriting exclusions for the very things they need healthcare for. Healthcare premiums for small companies have jumped at a double-digit rate. When you add that to the workers comp nightmares, the average citizens are in trouble. Those small business owners are the canaries in the mine of commerce. They aren't happy and have no where to go but to cut insurance entirely. You've seen what that did with the grocery strike here in Southern California."

"You're right. It's a mess and getting worse," Lee continued. "By 2006, those pesky experts out there say, premiums for a family, whether paid by the employer or the individual, could average more than $14,000 a year. Hey, the patients aren't happy; they're angry. The suppliers aren't happy, and the employers aren't happy with four years of double-digit growth in premiums. That means people are ready for a change."

"It's getting late, dear, so before *we* get unhappy, we're ready to hear *King Lee's* plan!" Kelly interrupted.

"By all means, your faithful subjects are ready for a proclamation," Lynn said, joining the fun.

"Bush has already said much of what I think needs to be done," Lee said, now a bit more humbly. "Government has to take an active role in reform, but its function ought not to be to centralize healthcare in Washington or to over-control the delivery of medicine. Bush wants healthcare costs to be more affordable and wants to give people more choices, not any one-size-fits-all approach."

"That sounds like a campaign sound byte," John said.

"OK, specifics. First, just like we require drivers in most states to show evidence of auto insurance, we require mandatory basic healthcare coverage," Lee said.

"Mandatory?" Lynn said. "What if they don't get coverage? Not all drivers get insurance."

"The legal drivers do," Lee replied. "Bush hasn't said this, but some have suggested that we need a system to hold people accountable. Those unable to prove insurance on their annual tax form could be automatically enrolled in a default private plan. The funds would be taken out of any refund, or the citizen would be billed. They would have to pay the bill or send in proof of enrollment in another approved plan."

"What about the 41 million who can't afford that coverage now?" Lynn asked. "You said earlier that many Americans don't even pay any taxes."

"They would get less of a refund. Look, not all of those 41 million without coverage can't afford it," Lee said. "They choose not to. Many are young; two thirds are below the age of 35. Most are middle class with

> *"In the book of life, the answers are not in the back."*
> *–Charles Schultz*

a third having annual incomes of more than $50,000. Most aren't poor. They just don't feel they need it, and would rather risk it and spend their money on other things. But if those relatively healthy and young citizens were forced to purchase a basic plan, the risk pool is decreased and it drives down the price all have to pay. Insured patients don't rely on expensive emergency rooms to get care. They would get better treatment and have peace of mind that they have coverage that won't be taken away. As I said earlier, we will need to subsidize that basic plan premium for the truly poor. President Bush, when he talked about healthcare change, proposed new tax credits for the poor so they can afford health coverage, up to $1,000 for an individual or $3,000 for a family."

"What about pre-existing conditions?" Lynn asked.

"That's the beauty of mandatory coverage," Lee continued. "Insurers would have to agree to accept all comers within their insured pool. With everyone in the pool we can afford treating those with pre-existing conditions. By getting in early and allowing the person to own their own basic policy for a lifetime, people won't have to worry about portability. It is their policy for a lifetime. You won't have to read about people being wiped out by that one serious uncovered medical illness."

"That sounds good," John said. "But to be cheap enough to afford there would have to be a very high deductible."

"You're right," Lee said. "This mandatory coverage

would not be a Cadillac plan. It would be a basic, no frills major medical coverage to protect people from catastrophic medical problems. After a certain preset, annual deductible amount, all costs would be paid. But this policy wouldn't cover all medical expenses. What we need is a *simple policy*. Unfortunately, legislators at both the state and federal level have pushed the price of individual and group plans out of the reach of most citizens by mandating coverage for all kinds of services—drug abuse, chiropractors, and acupuncturists. I think we should leave those costs for individuals to pay for."

"How do they pay for that?" Lynn asked.

"They'd pay for healthcare services through personal medical accounts. A Medical Savings Account, or MSA, allows citizens to make pre-tax contributions to an interest-bearing account," Lee continued. "When minor medical needs arise, the holder writes a check from that account to pay for what is needed. In some years, people won't use all the funds set aside, allowing people to roll those funds forward for future healthcare needs. With clarifications this year by the Treasury Department, the MSA accounts linked to a qualifying high-deductible health insurance are now a reality. Now, it's voluntary but available. The minimum deductible is $1,000 for individuals and $2,000 for families. As of now, the maximum people can deposit in the accounts is $2,600 for individuals and $5,150 for families. The deposits and earnings are tax-deferred. To qualify, the insurance linked to the accounts must require the consumer to pay the deductible first, but they have now exempted that rule for some preventive care—things like physicals, immunizations, and obesity treatment. The coverage can now be purchased by the individual or by employers."

"Sounds complicated," John said.

"It doesn't have to be," Lee continued. "Some are trying to put together cash-value insurance vehicles that would allow people to have one policy that contains both their medical account and pays their major medical premium. They would write checks out of the accumulated cash value. The money not used would just accumulate within the plan at a controlled interest rate."

"That might work," John responded. "That kind of product could be created, but Republicans talk about market pressure being effective in bringing down costs. How will the average consumers have the information they need to be smart healthcare shoppers?"

"Good question! When they pay out of their own funds instead of just handing them a plastic card someone else pays, they will ask about choices from their doctor and expect them to have options," Lee said. "If they don't get the right choices, they will go online to find information on cost and quality. We have websites to get the best price for most products. Why not websites for healthcare services and doctors? Just this year Medicare added price information on 60,000 specific drugs sold in nearly 75,000 pharmacies. You put in your zip code at www.medicare.gov and you get price comparison data on brand-name drugs and their generic equivalents. Competition and demand can expect to bring sites online that will have people identify their location and the specialization area needed. Medical treatment choices will then appear with patient ratings and costs. That will happen because that is what capitalistic competition creates whenever it is free to operate. There is too much price-fixing in healthcare now. We will need to let the market operate. Competition will allow value to surface. It's that same pressure that will cause consumers to use generic drugs when generics will do the job for less. Now, we just spend for the newest drug when other, cheaper drugs would do just fine. The key point is that the consumer can make the choices that impact their care because they have control of the money."

"What about employees whose companies pay for their coverage?" John asked.

"First of all, I have a bias. Corporations should no longer be given tax deductions for giving healthcare benefits to their workers," Lee said. "The money now used to fund the healthcare benefits should be given directly to employees, and that money should be recorded as income to those employees. Let the employee receive the tax deduction for *their own* healthcare policy choices. That way they get to choose the plan and the options they want and won't be limited by what an employer chooses to provide. It gives them far more control."

"Won't corporations fight this," John said.

"Yes and no! With the healthcare costs spiraling, they may be open to change," Lee continued. "Before World War II, people paid their own medical bills, just as they paid their rent or mortgage payment, bought their own food, and paid for whatever else they wanted. After World War II, the government imposed wage and price controls. Companies who wanted to hire and reward good employees were forbidden to offer higher wages, but they could offer health insurance coverage and call it a business expense instead of a wage. Today, as a result, most medical treatments are paid by third parties, employer-funded insurance or government insurance. The people who are *paying for* the care are not the people who are *using it*. The people using it have gotten used to a level of entitlement that we never had before. It used to work in attracting and keeping the best employees. Today, some people stay for those benefits when the company would rather they leave. I'm not sure if corporations are so eager to fight for funding benefits today. The current situation isn't working, and employees feel they are entitled to care the employers can no longer afford. After all, employers don't provide auto or homeowner's insurance."

"Are you seeing evidence of this?" John asked.

"Many large corporations are now providing or planning to provide similar defined-contribution plans where employees fund an employee's personal-care account for use on any standard medical procedure or medication. The annual allowance, voucher or account is usually funded with $1,000 to $2,000 for families and about half that for individuals," Lee explained. "After those funds are used in any given year, the employees are responsible for payments up to a preset ceiling for the year. Then an insurance plan covers any further expenses."

"That sounds like the Bush drug relief plan for Medicare," Lynn observed.

"They are both based on a similar model," Lee said. "Any funds not used in a given year are often rolled over into the next year. If the employee leaves the company and has money left in that account, the employee gets to take that money."

"Will drugs be covered under this plan of yours?" John asked.

"They need to be. Drugs used to be ancillary to treatment," Lee said. "Today, expensive but necessary drug treatments are the treatment of choice for many problems. We have to include drugs in any fair plan."

"You're forgetting the 'vitality points' you told me about last week," Kelly added. "Some of the companies give points for a more healthful lifestyle. If they quit smoking or go into weight-loss programs, they get 'vitality points' that can increase the interest rate on their patient-care account reserves or earn a discount on a health club membership. It rewards those who work to promote their own health. It gives people some power."

"Won't genuinely sick people forgo treatment because they want to pocket the money in their account?" Lynn asked.

"I suppose that is possible," Lee confessed. "But when I'm sick, I want to be fixed. Now, if they are using their funds, it might cause them to go to a clinic before going to an expensive emergency room. That would be progress! We're talking about giving people the power to get care but to be concerned about not spending as much money. The key point is that when it's their money, they think about that choice."

"Couldn't this be done with one-centralized government program?" John asked.

"It could, but centralized health planning is not what America needs," Lee said. "It doesn't respond to the individual needs of the patient. Centralized controls focus on cutting costs not giving you and me choices. When people control their own dollars, whether through their own accounts or tax credits, they can purchase health care that best suits their needs. Competition for providers helps improve healthcare quality and helps control costs. Putting individuals in control minimizes bureaucratic hassles for the citizens and the healthcare providers."

"Won't the insurance companies and the pharmaceuticals still be in a position to increase costs whenever they want to?" Lynn asked.

"Too many patients feel trapped by the system, with decisions about their health dictated by HMOs or government bureaucracies. Too many doctors feel buried in paperwork. I've heard it said that some doctors feel they don't practice medicine, they practice insurance." –George W. Bush

"Controls and ground-rules will still need to be in place. I think we will need to hold the line on drug patent periods so that generics drugs will become available quicker," Lee said. "Many don't expect Republicans to fight for patients over big business, but I think all Americans want to see fairness. There is too much patent gaming going on now. We know that generics reduce drug prices by 80% on average within three years on the market. We need that kind of savings working for our system."

"Won't that cut the profits of those pharmaceuticals that we need to invest in new drugs?" John asked.

"When they are allowed to get a profit for new drugs, their return on investment is good," Lee said. "But patients need to know that there is a limit to the protection that a patent provides. Having limits on a patent just encourages them to create more new drugs."

"These changes will also help curtail administrative costs," Kelly shared.

"How?" Lynn asked.

"The U.S. spends over $1,000 per person on health administration costs," Kelly continued. "Canada spends just over $300 per patient. With over 9,000 healthcare plans in California alone, that means 9,000 different sets of paperwork and record-keeping requirements. Standardized forms and record keeping is critical. That can be accomplished with authorizing simpler plans. There will be many insurance companies still competing for the business, but the common administrative standards can still be used to minimize costs."

"I also think we need a much more efficient information exchange available for healthcare agencies and physicians," Lee said. "More than 30 years ago, competing banks formed the VISA credit card collaborative and, together with merchants, created a real-time private financial information exchange at the point of service. It works. We need the same thing for healthcare. With people having no fear of losing coverage, there would be no fear of having a medical information exchange network available at the point of service. There would be no separate forms for each doctor, no fear that you would have no information available if you have an accident or need surgery on vacation. The information would be available and accurate—available to those *you* authorize to use. Electronic data and networked systems make this possible. Some see savings of up to $40 billion with this kind of system, not to mention the improvement in care and the drop in medical errors. With that kind of information, there are research implications that can isolate best practices and create quality improvements we can all benefit from."

"Lee wants to be one of the first to have his medical information put on a chip and implanted into his body," Kelly said.

"You're kidding?" Lynn said.

"No, she's right," Lee confessed. "I travel a lot. I want that information accessible and with me. Hey, they put information in dogs; I want it for me. I'd love to have an implanted data chip that can be updated by wireless transfer. I mean that's technology at its best when and where they need it."

"You need help," Lynn said laughing.

"That insures I will *get that help*," Lee said, joining in the laughter.

"Will all this information help with the 100,000 estimated patients who die each year in America from preventable medical errors?" John asked.

"That number is in question, but it has been reported," Lee said. "But, yes. This should help. Information systems promise that clinical decision-support, bar-coding and e-prescribing can help cut down on many of those medical errors. When you can't read a doctor's prescription, errors can result. An integrated information network will help make sure that doesn't happen. Right now practices vary too much across hospitals and regions. This will help standardize care; doctors will be asked to have a good explana-

"For the first time, all Americans will be responsible and held accountable for purchasing a basic level of health insurance. All Americans will have, at a minimum, a basic insurance package, defined by the federal government and similar to the standard benefit packages available to federal employees. ... For the first time, all Americans will be guaranteed access to group rate insurance, similar to the Federal Employee Health Benefit Program, where federal employees are pooled together, and the government negotiates the lowest possible premiums and offers a menu of health-plan options."
–Senator John Breaux

tion as to why they will change that care."

"How does that help?" Lynn asked.

"They used to use a straight-edge shaver for surgery preparation, but they found that the skin abrasion just increased the likelihood of infection," Lee said. "Now, they use decision-support to make sure proper procedures are used. Infections are down and quality of care is up because that best-practice research was shared."

"That makes sense to share that kind of information," Lynn said.

"When people have portability and continuity of care, patients will be more comfortable with information systems that can support this kind of system," Kelly stressed. "People are more concerned about privacy of medical data when that data can be used to *keep them from being insured.* That would no longer be the case with mandatory coverage that they own for life."

"Now, while I am king for the day, there are a couple of other problems worth changing," Lee said. "One of the biggest is the need for medical malpractice tort reform."

"*This change* is not going to be popular with many Democrats," Lynn said.

"I can understand," Lee said. "The lawyers are one of the top contributors to the Democrats in every election, and there is a reason for those contributions. The Democrats block tort reform at every level. The skyrocketing prices for medical malpractice insurance in some states are causing doctors to leave the profession. Doctors are even going on strike over it in some states. The excessive lawsuits are driving up the cost for everyone."

"Excessive is in the eye of the beholder," Lynn said. "Someone needs to be held accountable."

"Accountability is good, but excessive awards punish the people who pay for healthcare, not the doctors or professionals who made the mistake," Lee added. "That means you and me, the tax payers and policy holders who pay the bills! We need national legislation to cap the awards for pain and suffering. When awards are capped at less than $500,000, malpractice insurance costs are almost 25% less. Republicans want a lower cap; Democrats want a higher one or none at all. Look, we can argue about the limit, but we need limits. Actual costs would have no limit; we just need to limit the pain and suffering awards that public juries love to assign. We need a sane limit."

"I agree with that," John said. "It goes back to the victim thinking we talked about earlier. I'm tired of people suing for everything."

"I was laying it a little rough on the Democrats," Lee confessed. "I would be remiss not to say that Senator John Breaux, the Democratic Senator from Louisiana, has been a real work horse and visionary in this area. Unfortunately, he's retiring, but he's been fighting along side Senator Frist to make something happen in healthcare reform."

"That's good to hear," John said. "It's also good to hear you say that. Some issues ought to be able to be handled in a less partisan manner."

"I agree. I also think some of that nonpartisan brainstorming is needed in another area. The illegal immigration problem we face here in California and in many of our states is impacting our healthcare as well," Lee said. "Texas and California complain about not being able to take care of citizens, but part of the problem is that taxes are going to subsidize illegal aliens who have broken our laws in even coming here. Hospitals are forced to provide treatment, and we *all* pay the cost."

"Is it that big of a cost?" Lynn said.

"I read an article about the cost of caring for illegal immigrants in Colorado," Kelly said. "Colorado taxpayers paid the hospital bills for 6,000 illegal aliens who had their babies in Colorado at a cost of $5,000 per baby. Those 6,000 births to illegal aliens were 40 percent of the births paid for by Medicaid in Colorado. Those 6,000 babies immediately became U.S. citizens and qualified for Medicaid services. To get that care, the mother only has to say she is 'undocumented.' American mothers can't get out of *their hospital costs* quite so easily."

"That doesn't seem fair," Lynn confessed.

"That's just part of the story," Lee said.

"Before we all begin to fade," Kelly said. "I think we better get to that last topic, how to deal with the illegal immigrant problem."

"Nothing like ending on a tough one," Lee said. "This topic usually leaves me tossing and turning. But I'd love to hear your thoughts on this as well. There are so many great Hispanic American citizens who are a tribute to our country. It's a difficult issue to talk about without stirring up a lot of emotions."

"I'm sure you will try," John said with a smile.

"I think we all need to try to find a workable answer, because this is one problem that is not going away easily," Lee said sighing.

Chapter Fourteen

The Immigration Challenge

"One of the primary reasons America became a great power in the 20th century is because we welcomed the talent and the character and the patriotism of immigrant families. We must make our immigration laws more rational and more humane. And I believe we can do so without jeopardizing the livelihoods of American citizens."
–George W. Bush

★ ★ ★

"OK, I'm waiting to hear your Republican ideas about our immigration problem," John said with focus. "The Bush temporary guest worker program continues to get hit from the right and the left. It may help in the election on Tuesday, but to most it's just election-year window dressing. I heard one Hispanic commentator call it *piñata politics*! It looks pretty dangling it out there, but it won't deliver what it promises."

"There are some good things there and some problems," Lee said. "Even with the witching hour fast approaching, let me take a brief but important tangent."

"Very brief," Kelly said. "I hope."

"Compassionate liberals love to send that letter that describes the world if it were a village and how the five richest citizens would be Americans and most of the rest would be poor," Lee said quickly.

"Yeah, I've seen that," Lynn said. "I always feel bad when I read that. It goes around the Internet at least once a year."

"That is the feeling they want us to have," Lee said. "Instead of being a tribute to our values, our free enterprise system and the drive of our people, they want you to feel bad for the poor around the world as if it were our fault for making them that way."

"Spreading the wealth is important," Lynn continued.

"That's what they would like you to believe," Lee said. "But when it comes to free trade, those same liberals scream bloody murder over the loss of American jobs to any of those same *poor* countries in that *world village* they talk about."

"How does this relate to our immigration problem?" John asked.

"Republicans want this immigration problem to go away," Lee confessed. "Bush has proposed a moderate plan, and they have held hearings. But they don't even list the issue on their donation surveys. They want to use it to get more Hispanic votes, but they don't want it to even be on the radar screen with the Republican base. It's like everyone is paralyzed by a crazy combination of anger and resentment over the invasion of illegals mixed with guilt, pity and compassion for the very people who are coming."

"That doesn't sound like much of a solution," John said.

"Precisely," Lee agreed. "The Republicans find themselves immobilized in inaction. We don't call them *illegal immigrants*. Most supporters of change call them *undocumented* taking all hint of lawbreaking out of the label."

"If Republicans do speak up against illegal immigrants, they are labeled *racist, xenophobic* or worse," Kelly added. "I know, because I'm not known for silence on this issue. But those politicians who are in office prefer to settle for silence, because they firmly believe it is not the reason people vote for or against them."

"And the Democrats?" John asked.

"The Democrats have their own problems," Lee said. "They just yell at the Republicans for not caring enough to fix the problem. To them, the Bush approach is a cynical, political ploy that helps employers far more than undocumented workers. The only solution Democrats have is amnesty so that people can vote for Democrats quicker! But they know that angers their labor base. Labor knows that such a plan would lower wages. As far as the unions are concerned, there would be plenty of Americans ready to work these jobs if the jobs paid better. So Kerry and the Democrats don't talk too loud on this either, and when they do speak up, they talk out of both sides of their mouths."

"Neither one of you are *silent* Republicans," John persisted. "What solutions do you suggest?"

"I'll let Kelly speak for herself because we don't agree on this issue either," Lee said with feeling. "I do know we agree

> *"Immigration from Mexico was once as measured and legal as it is now uncontrolled and unlawful. And instead of meeting the challenge of turning illegal immigrants into Americans, our teachers, politicians and government officials for some time have taken the easier route of allowing a separatist culture, from bilingualism and historical revisionism in the schools to non-enforcement of legal statues and a general self-imposed censorship about honest discussion of the problem."*
> *–Victor Davis Hanson*

on the long-range solution, and we both hope it is a vision that Mexico shares. America should do everything possible to strengthen the *Mexican Dream!* We need to help Mexico foster a social, political and economic infrastructure that will make Mexico a prosperous neighbor. Better-paying jobs help reduce poverty and would eventually stem the need for illegal immigration."

"That's your answer?" Lynn asked.

"It's the most important one," Lee said. "As long as the disparity of opportunity is so great between our two countries, the gate will always swing northward. No one can blame them for wanting more for their families. These people risk their lives coming here. Most of them work hard. Most are not beggars. If they beg for anything, they beg for work!"

"What did you say in your presentation?" John said. "The biggest difference between a vision and a hallucination is the number of people who can see it. There is a big gap between your vision and current reality in Mexico."

"I admit that is true," Lee said. "It doesn't change the importance of the vision. And, even over the last few tough economic years, objective indicators in Mexico have improved. There is low inflation, growing investment, rising incomes and a better debt structure. The Bush-backed Central American Free Trade Agreement now is solidifying that support from Canada to the tip of South America."

"All is not rosy in any of those countries," John continued. "America used to be able to count on a rubber stamp from them, but not anymore. When Bush went into Iraq, less than a third of the Latin American and Caribbean nations supported the war. Next to our relationship with France, no relationship was damaged more by the war than our relationship with Mexico."

"True, that was a real setback in the relationship between Bush and Fox," Lee said. "But there are more problems for Fox than just a strained relationship. Job growth remains static, and corruption remains a major problem. Mexicans are used to a powerful, domineering PRI President. Fox came in promising change, but he has had to share power with a very difficult Congress dominated by hostile parties in both the lower and upper houses. He thought he'd get a boost from Bush with his amnesty request. Then 9/11, and then the rift over the Iraq war. If you think Bush has problems, try being in Fox's shoes!"

"Then why do you have hope in your solution?" John said.

"Because we need to sell Americans on the importance of helping our neighbors to the south," Lee said. "We either help them improve so that people can stay in their homeland to find opportunity, or millions of immigrants will keep coming. We have to work for change no matter how long it takes. I saw a political cartoon that had a husband talking to his wife about the Bush guest worker program. He observed, 'Eventually, illegal workers won't need amnesty…Because they can return to their country and have our jobs.' In some segments of our economy that will be true, and I think *that is good*. It will force people here to retool and refocus to find new careers and new businesses. That kind of change is healthy. Besides, when Mexico and Central America are more prosperous, there is an added benefit—there will be more customers who can afford American products and services."

"You're vision isn't popular with the unions *or* conservatives," Lynn said.

"Bingo," Lee said. "It won't be popular unless it is sold properly. I've written Bush on this foreign policy issue a number of times."

"Does he write back?" Lynn asked.

"Not on this," Lee said laughing. "Look, it shouldn't just be the U.S. As Kelly said earlier, the U.N. is useless as a united force in fighting evil or in promoting a strong world economy. Bush challenged the U.N. before the Iraq war. It was March 2003, in front of the U.N. when Bushed asked, 'Are Security Council resolutions to be honored and enforced, or cast aside without consequence? Will the United Nations serve the purpose of its founding, or will it be irrelevant.' As we all know, they chose to be irrelevant, and, once again, a coalition of the willing was required to go to war to enforce their own resolutions. The United Nations is simply incapable of acting strongly in cases of serious disagreement among the five countries possessing veto power over decisions of the Security Council. It isn't any better in promoting freedom and economic vitality."

"So why not withdraw?" John asked. "I am not that impressed with them either."

"No, as we said earlier, it still serves a purpose. Many conservatives would love the U.S. to withdraw from the U.N.," Lee continued. "I think that would be a mistake and waste energy, money, and Bush's already rocky international political capital. The U.S. should stay involved but limit our monetary commitment and work to limit the scope of the U.N. mission to what it does well. The U.N. can collect and distribute humanitarian aid. They can settle disputes among smaller nations where U.N. mediations and even U.N. 'peacekeeping' forces might be possible and helpful. The U.N. also remains the only central forum where the world's countries, including the smaller ones without large foreign ministries, can gather to debate, negotiate, and exchange views. But such functions are limited and deserve limited resources and limited expectations. Keep the U.N., but don't expect much."

"So what is your answer?" John pressed. "This is a long tangent!"

"Bush is used to working in building coalitions," Lee said. "It's time to form an organization. What did Kelly call it?"

"The United Freedom Alliance, U.F.A.," Kelly responded.

"That's as good a label as any," Lee continued. "We'd work to create a coalition of free countries committed to democratic principles, freedom, capitalism and the rule of law. Its mission would be to foster and support those principles and target foreign aid to developing countries like Mexico that are committed to make democracy, capitalism and freedom work."

"You'd limit the membership?" John asked.

"You bet I would," Lee said. "There would be no Human Rights Commission headed by Libya or by Cuba. There would be no votes by totalitarian regimes, because they would not be members of U.F.A. If countries are not putting democratic ideals to work for freedom and prosperity, they wouldn't be able to join and they shouldn't expect foreign aid from us. It's time to take a stand for democracy and freedom, and Bush is the leader to do just that."

"He hasn't written you back," Kelly confessed.

"The idea must be percolating," Lee laughed. "Hey, these are Republican principles. The *American Dream* should never be limited to any one country. President Bush has said it many times that it is a God given right for every world citizen to be free, and I agree with that."

"Ah, another good political sound byte," Lynn said.

"It actually sounds more religious to me," Lee confessed. "But the fact remains that democracy and freedom are making headway in the world. Communism is defeated. Iraq still has its moments, but there is now a real beachhead for freedom right in the heart of the Middle East. Prior to 1985, less than 40% of the world's population was served by democratic governments. After 2000, that number was nearly 60% and growing. We should be putting our support and foreign aid dollars into expanding that effort, not funding tyranny."

"OK, that is progress and I appreciate your vision for Mexico and the U.F.A.," John continued. "But this vision isn't going to deal with the problem we face today. And Mexico is not the only immigration problem we have."

"You're right. The immigration problem is down-right

dangerous," Kelly added. "Seventeen-year-old John Lee Malvo who joined John Allen Muhammad on that 23-day shooting rampage was an illegal alien. Malvo and his mother were stowaways on a cargo ship from Jamaica."

"I don't think I've read that," Lynn said.

"The media doesn't dwell on what it doesn't want to say," Kelly said. "Malvo and his mom were arrested in the state of Washington in a custody dispute. Neither had papers proving citizenship. The Border Patrol recommended that they be deported. The I.N.S. held them a month and let them loose. Both 9/11 and the Beltway sniper were failures of our government and our collective will to control our borders. As stowaways, Malvo and his mom should have been deported without a hearing. They weren't."

"You remember the California campaign for Proposition 187," Lee said. "And you remember the result—an overwhelming approval."

"Of course," John said. "I think it would pass again. I would vote for it."

"I think you're right," Kelly said. "Most Californians know the cost illegal aliens bring to California, not to mention the other states. As we mentioned earlier, the healthcare cost to treat undocumented aliens is devastating. Add to that the fact that over 30 percent of all illegal-immigrant households receive benefits from at least one welfare program. The average welfare payment—just counting the four major welfare programs—to illegal immigrant households is $1,400 a year. This just adds to the California budget deficit. Half of all kids in the public-school system are from immigrant families. They may pay taxes, but half of immigrants are too poor to pay any income tax."

"That's upsetting," John confessed.

"That's not all," Kelly said. "Some advocates now want the U.S. government to provide retirement refunds for illegal aliens who used stolen or fake Social Security numbers."

"That isn't what Bush wants to do," Lee countered. "He's been very clear with his plan. His temporary guest workers would be protected by U.S. wage and workplace safety laws. They would be able to apply for green cards that would put them on a path to permanent status and possible citizenship, but there is no illusion that all would earn that. That's where the incentives come in, but they have structured it for them to leave, not stay. Guest workers would be able to open tax-free savings accounts that they could cash out when they *returned* to their homelands. The Social Security taxes they now would be paying would be credited to the workers under their countries' retirement systems. That way they don't have to pay into two systems. Sure it increases the number of people eligible for benefits but it also increases the number of guest workers and their employers that are paying taxes. Even more important, it gives the guest workers an incentive to go back home."

"Well, they deserve some benefits for the jobs they are doing. They do jobs Americans won't do," Lynn said. "The real reason they keep coming is that there are employers ready to hire them, and you can't tell me they don't know they're illegal!"

"That's always said," Lee said. "And there is some truth to that, but it doesn't state the whole problem. Outside of oil, Mexico's greatest export is labor. Every day, a wave of humanity makes its way north with or without proper documentation. They come to do work that Americans *supposedly* won't do, or at least won't do at the prices Mexicans are willing to accept. They mow our lawns, cook our meals, build our buildings, raise our children, and clean our homes. Unfortunately, we just won't face the fact that what we are doing isn't working. As long as employers can get illegals to work for them at a rock-bottom price, they will not hire Americans willing to work at a slightly higher wage. It's the low-skilled domestic workers, minorities and our legal immigrants that get hurt the most."

"In what way?" Lynn asked.

"I don't often report on studies from the UCLA Chicano Studies Research Center," Lee said with a smile. "But they found that native Americans and legal immigrants in the United States earn 11 percent less when they work with new Hispanic immigrants. Minority workers are hit the hardest. They earn an average of 14 percent less. The more new immigrants there are, the less the other American workers make. That's why the big employers love our open borders. It effectively rolls back the minimum-wage law that unions love to get the Democrats to pass."

"So you are going to send back millions of illegals," Lynn said. "And how are you going to do that?"

"I didn't say that," Lee said. "I'm closer to Bush on this."

"You support his temporary worker plan?" Lynn pushed.

"I do with some reservations," Lee said.

"I have more than some reservations," Kelly added. "Lee and I have different opinions about the plan."

"I'll let Kelly share her thoughts, but I support Bush's plan because of some stark realities. Some put the number of undocumented aliens at 6 million; others say there are as many as 14 million illegals," Lee mused. "So let's get real. No one has the political will to deport that many people. So as much as people hate to reward illegal immigration, Americans wouldn't stand for uprooting that many people. Many of these undocumented aliens have woven their lives into the fabric of communities. In some towns in California, they are the majority of the population. When there is a pregnant or injured illegal at a hospital, we aren't going to transport them to a plane and send them back. If a child is hungry, we aren't going to refuse to feed them. It would take a bureaucracy and resources Americans will not tolerate— thousands of lawyers, immigration police and transportation requisitions. No, we have to be willing to try something new."

"I'm glad to hear you say that," Lynn said.

"Kelly is not as glad as you are, but Bush has tried to find a compassionate and workable middle path," Lee continued. "He's said many times that he doesn't believe in a blanket amnesty program. There should be no 'automatic path to citizenship for foreigners who are in the United States illegally.' I think he's right that America is a welcoming country but there should be no automatic reward for violating our laws."

"Vicente Fox and the amnesty advocates here in the states want far more than Bush is willing to promise, and they are going to keep pushing," Kelly added. "The only acceptable version of 'immigration reform' to them is a blanket amnesty. Fox wants the illegals living in America to be given U.S. citizenship and still have them continue to vote in Mexican elections and send money back to their relatives. Fox is desperate; he's lost over 25 percent of his party's seats in the Mexican Congress. Only a divide in the PRI party is giving him a little time. He wants grateful U.S. illegals to give him their votes in the next election. If he gets them legal, permanent status or citizenship, they'll vote for him if they can."

"Making life easy for illegals is political suicide for Republicans." John said. "Your base won't go for it."

"Tell me about that," Kelly said. "I'm not happy about the Bush plan as it stands now. I can't get over the fact that this further undermines the rule of law. People need to wait their turn. You can dance around this, but it's legalizing people who came here illegally. They cut in line."

"Many Democrats would even be mad if there is a blanket amnesty program," John continued.

"I told you, Lee," Kelly added. "We are selling our country away for cheaper meals, manicured gardens and prettier greens. If they didn't have the illegals working for them, they would have to pay more or use machines to do the work. People would then make their own choice."

"Blanket amnesty is not the answer," Lee said. "But there are no easy answers. Bush has invested a lot of political capital in even proposing a plan. In the current situation, the understaffed

I.N.S. just tries to focus on stopping the coyotes from smuggling people across the border. They raid a few sweatshops every time U.S. workers are displaced. Congress passes more laws for show, knowing that I.N.S. is incapable of enforcing those laws. So we have millions upon millions of people who are breaking the laws of our country, but it remains business as usual. That's why I was glad Bush put something on the table to work with."

"Guest worker programs don't work," Kelly said. "Europe's guest worker programs created more problems than they solved. Most of the several million Turks and Yugoslavs in Germany are there because of past guest worker programs. Germany's program ended two decades ago. There's a growing Muslim population. These past workers get some benefits, but they are not citizens. They found out the hard way that most guest workers aren't good guests; they stay. They marry locals, have children, and they encourage other family members to come, legally or illegally. The guest workers aren't forced to go home, but no one knows what to do with them. You would be hard pressed to find anyone today who would want to bring those guest worker programs back. They just made things worse."

"If Kelly is right, why do you think Bush's plan would work better than the plans in Europe?" John asked.

"America is better than Europe in assimilating people who stay," Lee said. "Our melting pot still melts. It melts slowly, but it melts. The incentives I mentioned earlier will help get more to go home to Mexico. But I'll be honest, there are a lot of things to work out that are not clear yet."

"A *lot of things!*" Kelly said.

"I have a strong feeling that even Republicans disagree on this one," Lynn said. "Like the two who are sitting here with us now."

"That's perceptive," Lee said laughing. "But as I said before, there is room in this party for diversity of positions. There is even room in this household…I hope!"

"There is," Kelly said with a smile.

"We've talked about the problem," Lee said. "It's time we focus on a few solutions."

"Do our guests want sleep or solutions?" Kelly asked.

"Are you kidding," John said. "I don't want to have bad dreams about this problem."

"No, the reality is bad enough," Kelly confessed.

Chapter Fifteen

Searching for Immigration Solutions

"There is no American race; there is just an American creed." –George W. Bush

★ ★ ★

"OK, what are the high-points of Bush's plan?" Lee summarized. "As I understand it, the 'temporary worker program' would allow both illegal immigrants already in the United States or someone abroad to apply for the right to work legally in the country for a three-year term. Before hiring any foreign guest worker, the employer would have to advertise the job and show that no Americans wanted the job. Temporary worker applicants already in the United States would have to pay a yet-to-be-established registration fee and show they are currently employed. After three years, if they are still employed, they would be permitted to renew their permit. They haven't agreed with how many times the permit could be renewed. As an added plus, the guest workers with permits would be allowed to move freely back and forth between the U. S. and their home country."

"Do the guest workers applying from other countries have to pay a fee?" Lynn asked.

"No, legal applicants still in their home countries won't have to pay a fee," Lee answered. "But they will have to have a job lined up in America."

"How many temporary workers will they authorize?" John asked.

"Hey, the New England area could use a few guest workers," Kelly added. "But California already has a glut of workers at the low end and this plan just promises more. This program would grease the skid to lower wages by having even more workers."

"As of now, the President has set no limit on the number of temporary workers who could come, provided the jobs were not being filled by Americans," Lee said.

"Tell Congress that. Congress will never authorize the number needed to make more illegals sign up," Kelly said in frustration. "Even if they did, it would be a hollow promise. Too few are going to make it to permanent status. Some are already saying that it is a trap. With as many as 11 million illegals and as few as 200,000 green cards and even fewer citizenship opportunities, signing up as a guest worker for three years just insures you are more likely to be sent back. The line for green cards is already long! If you have been here and survived illegally for ten years, why risk everything now? When their temporary status runs out and they have no job, they are history. This doesn't offer them hope; it just offers them a temporary job."

"I agree. As it now stands, the channel leading to U.S. citizenship is very narrow," Lee conceded. "Bush has tried to lower expectations that guest workers would eventually become permanent residents, much less citizens."

'It's so narrow, it can't work," Kelly added. "The funnel from guest worker to green card is barely a drip. Neither Mexicans nor anyone else will go through the hassle and paperwork of seeking legal jobs as long as the chance of getting a green card is so minimal. Signing up just insures their deportation, not permanent status here. With the border still so porous and employers holding all the cards in whether to allow their workers to apply for a permit, they will just keep doing what they are doing. They won't have the people to find the abusers and prosecute them."

"What if he increased the number of green cards available?" Lynn asked.

"I think he should push for that," Lee agreed. "Kelly is right. If there is no hope, they won't apply."

"Republicans won't go for a blank number here," Kelly added.

"They are living here already," Lee said. "But you're right. Most Republicans won't support Bush on this unless they get something in return to appease their base."

"Bush and his happy employers out there want the guest workers' sweat and labor," Kelly added. "But, ultimately, they don't want *them*."

"I really think Bush feels it is the right thing to do," Lee said. "He wants to pull immigrants out of the shadows of American society under the protection of U.S. labor laws. He wants them to be able to travel freely back and forth to their home countries."

"I think Bush does believe that," Kelly said. "But not all conservatives define *compassionate* the way George Bush does. How would you win their support?"

"Bush would have to make sure that getting a green card was achievable but difficult," Lee added. "He'd have to make earning U.S. citizenship even more difficult."

"Citizenship has to mean something!" Lynn agreed.

"You're right!" Lee added. "Back to being king for a day, I'd require them to earn the right of citizenship by enduring a long probationary period where they build up a case for citizenship. If they have no criminal record, close family ties, a good employment history, tax compliance, and good progress toward learning English, they should be able to earn citizenship."

"I don't think it should be easy either," John confessed.

"That doesn't make you much of a Democrat," Lee said with a smile. "Clinton and Gore tried to get the wait time for citizenship naturalization from two years to two months."

"Nothing that easy is appreciated," Lynn said.

"Citizens should have to be competent in English," Kelly said nodding. "Learning English has to be an urgent priority. American citizens should not have to provide foreign language ballots. Speaking and reading English is *supposed* to be a requirement for becoming a citizen, and *only* citizens are eligible to vote. Today, in many cities, Latino immigrants live in their own sub-nation with their own radio and TV stations, newspapers, films, and magazines. The painful truth is that such openness stunts their assimilation and cuts down on their economic opportunity. We don't need to import a culture of poverty and disunity. If we do this, we need to help them embrace the *American Dream*."

> *"Supporting English as the national language, and encouraging immigrants to learn English, isn't anti-Hispanic or anti-immigrant. The only reason the United States has successfully integrated so many millions of immigrants over the last 150 years is precisely because we have a common language and culture." –Linda Chavez*

"You can't legislate what people speak in their homes," Lynn pushed back.

"Of course not," Lee said. "But my Swedish immigrant grandfather wouldn't allow Swedish to be spoken in the home. The children were expected to learn English. Today, political correctness and multiculturalism has made selling America an oppressive act! They undermine our heroes, history, achievement and language. In fact, it's the multiculturalists that stop us from making clear demands on what new immigrants must do to live up to citizenship."

"Thank goodness we have returned to English immersion here in California instead of bi-lingual education," John added.

"It should be much tougher than it is now," Kelly continued. "The citizenship is now little more than rote regurgitation of answers they are taught, and that is not what was intended. The citizenship statute says that a citizenship test must require a fundamental knowledge and understanding of history, the principles and forms of our U.S. government. As far as I'm concerned, citizenship should take at least five years so we can insure that there is strong transfer of common values and a common language."

"Some undocumented aliens are not interested in becoming Americans with our values and our language," Lynn said.

"You are absolutely right," Lee said. "They would be perfect for the guest worker program. They could also stay with a green card if they earned it. No one should be given U.S. citizenship unless they *want to become Americans*. In fact, dual citizenship really bothers me."

"It bothers me, too," John agreed.

"To become an American you are asked to 'absolutely and entirely renounce all allegiance' to any foreign state," Lee said. "That's very clear. But in Mexico, dual citizenship is very big. In fact, I'd hope that Bush would push hard in negotiations with Fox to repeal the Mexican law they passed in 1998 that reinstated Mexican nationality for Mexican-Americans who have become naturalized U.S. citizens. There is talk of allowing them to vote in America *and* in Mexico. I think people should make a choice."

"Look, we don't want to end up like Canada," Kelly said, "They have a divided culture that will never come together. We

181

don't need to end up with two divided cultures. It's happening today in parts of LA! For a radical minority, it's like they are taking back their land. They're trying to reverse the Mexican-American war one block at a time."

"What war?" Lynn asked.

"Americans have mostly forgotten about the 1847 Mexican-American War," Lee said. "Some Mexicans have not forgotten. America won the war and occupied Mexico for eleven months. The current border was fixed when the victors walked away with half of what was then Mexico."

"Texas and the Alamo?" Lynn asked.

"Yes, Texas," Lee explained. "But add California, New Mexico, Arizona, Nevada, Utah…and beyond. Americans see the quaint missions. Some radicals see their homeland occupied. Hey, most Mexican immigrants love our ideals of freedom, equality and opportunity, and now they are the biggest minority in America."

"Do you think they really want that land back?" John asked.

"Some do, but most of them don't even want to stay here," Lee confessed. "In fact, right now, many feel trapped by the very security designed to keep them out. Migrant workers who used to cross the border each spring from Mexico and returned south for the holidays at home are now more likely to stay because of the tight security. It's an unintended consequence. It's supposed to keep people out, but it does a better job of keeping them locked in. They are afraid they won't be able to get back in, so they stay taking odd jobs until the next crop. They used to return to their

> *"While you bring all countries with you, you come with the purpose of leaving all other countries behind you—bringing what is best of their spirit, but not looking over your shoulders and seeking to perpetuate what you intended to leave behind in them."*
> *–Woodrow Wilson*

Mexican homes for Christmas with money and gifts. Now they stay and send back the cash; some estimate that amount to be within 9 to 13 billion dollars. If they could cross legally without any problem, most would come one or two times a year. Many illegals want to reside in Mexico with their families."

"So, that's where the guest worker program would help," John continued.

"That's right! The Bush plan would save money and increase taxes," Lee said emphatically. "Guest workers would be expected to pay for services they now are mandated to receive for free without paying taxes. Their children may attend public schools, but only U.S. citizens living in California would receive in-state tuition fees at state universities. There would be no free healthcare. Just like Canadians who visit America often purchase 'snowbird' health insurance policies to cover costs should they need healthcare while in the United States, those in the guest worker programs would be required to have healthcare coverage, whether purchased in Mexico or here, whether paid for by the worker or the employer."

"Can it work in cutting down undocumented immigrants?" Lynn asked. "I hate the exploitation by the smugglers. I hate reading about the lost lives in the desert, the poor wages for long hours of work. We need a change."

"Hawaii has lots of jobs that on the mainland are held by illegal aliens, yet there is no illegal immigration problem in the land of the pineapple," Lee interjected. "In Hawaii, they bring in contract workers from other nations to do the harvesting. They come, they work, and they leave. The guest worker idea creates a similar path for contract workers, who come, work and leave."

"It's a long swim for illegals to get to Hawaii," John said. "There are miles of common borders with Mexico, and we can't watch every foot. The devil is in the details and the implementation with any program like this. It certainly didn't work too well when Reagan tried his amnesty program. I'm not sure it will do anything to stop the flow of illegals into this nation. I'm even less convinced that those illegals now in America will sign up, work and leave."

"That's my fear about this change. When President Reagan signed into law the Immigration Reform and Control Act of 1986, he offered amnesty and legal status to most illegal immigrants already living in the states," Kelly responded. "In the next four years, 2.7 million green cards were issued to illegal immigrants. Now, they tried to discourage future illegal entries by imposing penalties on the employers. We now know how effective that was! To avoid the penalties, employers asked for documents and illegals gave them faked documents. They both knew they didn't have the people to enforce the rules. Reagan's law was an invitation, not a deterrent. That's why so many have come. They hope that Bush will get a similar law passed so that they too can win in another citizenship lottery."

"That's why this has to be structured differently," Lee agreed. "I hope this guest worker program and a tough but achievable path to green card status and citizenship for those who work to earn it will be the first step to stop and even roll back this massive illegal immigration problem. I honestly believe that some will leave and some will stay. I hope for the right reasons."

"What about those who still come without papers?" Lynn asked. "When they can't get guest worker permits, the coyotes will still bring illegals into the U.S. in hopes of joining the party."

"Once caught, they would be deported," Lee continued. "With a guest worker program available, there would be more of a need to enforce illegal entry. They are now paying those coyotes a lot just to get here. If they had a legal option, I think many would use it and put up with the paperwork and the cost of coming legally."

"Do you think there is the will to pull this off?" John asked.

"I hope so. First, America is going to have to actually

follow through on deporting those who should be deported," Lee said. "I have heard that there are over 130,000 who have already received deportation orders but have evaded deportation. We need to develop a way to earn citizenship for those who are serious, get others into the guest worker program for the shorter-term laborers, and actually get tough on deporting those who should be deported. Many of these are convicted criminals. They should be the first to go."

"We agree on that," Kelly said. "It's time we make sure some deportations occur."

"There is another proposal I have that Kelly and I don't yet agree on," Lee said, looking at Kelly. "I believe it is time for a National ID that works as a driver's license and national identification for voting and other services. The prototypes they are looking at would have a fingerprint, a picture, retina scan and DNA coding."

"Big brother is looming," Kelly said cautiously.

"We need a reliable ID," Lee said. "As it is now, our driver's licenses end up being used as national IDs. Unfortunately, not all states are effective in screening the use of their licenses. Florida is where most of the terrorists implicated in the 9/11 attack got their licenses. We need uniform standards, and, whether Kelly likes it or not, most Americans support a national ID."

"Are such IDs really that reliable?" Lynn asked.

"They have scanners that can spot fake IDs by reading the bar codes on driver's licenses," Lee said.

"Yes, I read that article," Kelly interrupted. "When they use those machines, those Americans who you say want these IDs have called the people using the scanners 'ID Nazis' or 'ID Police.' It may work for awhile, but criminals will still find a way to beat the systems you create."

"That is no reason to make it easy to do so," Lee countered. "The national ID is a good start, and the information included would also help stop identity fraud."

"Dear, our Republican friends are disagreeing again," Lynn said.

"It's an endearing quality we have to our relationship," Lee said. "Now, whether I have to sleep in the other room tonight is another matter."

"No, you can still sleep with me. Republicans can handle a few disagreements," Kelly said. "That is if we *ever finish* this dinner conversation."

"No one is yawning yet," Lee said. "Besides we can't stay with the system we have now. You have the undocumented clamoring for driver's licenses. Mexico wants to make money issuing matricula consular cards as IDs and wants America to accept them for IDs. To get one, all their people have to provide is a Mexican birth certificate, an official picture ID, proof of a local U.S. address and $29. They want them to be able to use the cards to cross the border and in airline travel. But we have no control over the validity and reliability of these cards. We do accept passports and Congress wisely passed the Enhanced Border Security and Visa Entry Reform Act which requires a computerized database of information on prospective visitors including biometric data, eye scans and fingerprints. We need to stand firm on that."

"As far as I'm concerned, the matricula consular card is stealth amnesty, a *let's pretend ID* designed to give undocumented aliens access to U.S. privileges and benefits to which they currently are not entitled," Kelly contested.

"That's why we need a better ID process and controls," Lee said. "With a valid passport, a guest worker card or a green card for people on the way to citizenship, people ought to be able to get a driver's license. But, no matter who the person, to get that license, people will have to show evidence of insurance coverage, have fingerprints and retinal scans and, then, have a criminal check. I don't think Governor Schwarzenegger is going to be quick to sign any driver's license legislation without stronger safeguards and background checks."

"And he shouldn't sign it," Kelly responded.

"Well, I agree with Lee," Lynn said. "Something has to be done to get formal IDs. Now, you have undocumented drivers who don't have insurance and are getting into traffic accidents. No one wants to reward people for breaking immigration laws and provide terrorists with easier access to drivers' licenses. But it's humiliating when an illegal is pulled over randomly for a check and they have no license. Then their car, their only means of transportation, is taken away from them, and their families are left on the sidewalk. That's terrible."

"Immigrants don't need to have California driver's licenses to drive legally," Lee added. "If immigrants who are here legally as guest workers want to drive legally in the US, all they need is their Mexican, Central American or South American driver's licenses. Now, they still must follow the insurance and other driving laws of California and the United States. We allow cars and trucks with Mexican license plates into this country as long as they show the proper papers. The same is true for driving. That is why I don't think California, or any state for that matter, should allow illegal immigrants the same rights as a legal, documented, green-card holder who worked very hard to gain access legally to the United States?"

"I agree, and I also think the national IDs and better controls are good," John added. "But I think we need to do more to hold employers accountable for hiring illegals. If enforced, a crackdown and fines would change the economic advantage of hiring the undocumented workers. They even fined Wal-Mart last year. Maybe that is a step in the right direction."

"Yes, they fined Wal-Mart," Lee said. "They studied it for five years and then swept in for show. They wanted to set an example, but it was still done with a wink and a nod. The low-cost workforce is what they want. Wal-Mart and others use subcontractors to pass the blame and hide direct accountability.

Documents can be forged easily; so they can check and illegals will still be hired. Proving an employer really knew is hard to do."

"The truth is that we don't fine employers now," Kelly added. "I read that over 200,000 businesses are believed to employ undocumented workers and just over 50 are fined in a given year. And with the budget cuts and money going elsewhere, there are fewer agents looking into it."

"The businesses hiring these men and women push for the *rights of immigrants* to work in America," Lee said. "But they don't push for real change. What they want is a steady supply of low-cost employees to continue. If Bush's plan to actually create guest worker programs and more in the green card citizen pipeline actually happens, many are not going to like it. Because, when they have a legal status, they are going to demand higher wages. When they do that, some American citizens may actually apply. None of these are simple answers, but we need to make progress on sorting out a plan and start implementing it. And as Kelly has so eloquently argued, if we don't deport those that deserve to be deported, we will lose all credibility and just encourage more illegal crossings."

"There is something else we need to do here," Kelly added.

"What is that?" Lynn asked.

"If we get an actual guest-worker program and a true track for those with green cards to earn citizenship, it is time we reject or, if need be, repeal the policy of children born to visiting immigrants becoming citizens of the U.S. automatically." Kelly replied. "We need to do away with

> *"In the past, people came here to become Americans, not remain foreigners. But between the multicultural craze and the proximity to Mexico, Americanization has an uphill fight and may never become the norm."*
> *–Thomas Sowell*

188

automatic *Advance to Go* ticket to citizenship when a child of illegals or guest workers is born in the U.S. Now, it is a strong incentive for illegals to risk crossing the border. And having a baby born here shouldn't create an inside track for relatives living elsewhere to come here legally."

"I actually agree, and a tough stance on this would bring many conservatives on board," Lee added. "Although the 14th Amendment states that all persons born or naturalized in the United States are citizens of the United States, there are persuasive arguments that the custom of blanket birthright citizenship is supported neither by the 14th Amendment nor by legal precedent. Let's stop demeaning citizenship by accepting *happy accident* Americans who just happened to be born here while their mothers are visiting. We go back to the key point—citizenship should be earned by people willing to work to earn it!"

"I'm still not sure that tackling this problem is ever going to be faced by either party," John said. "Bob Dole ran on a platform that called for an amendment to deny citizenship to children born in the U.S. of illegal immigrants. It didn't work for him."

"That was Bob Dole. In 1994, Proposition 187 was passed by just under 60 percent of the popular vote," Lee said. "Now, it was killed by the courts, but I think it is a myth that it was poison to the Republican Party. Arnold Schwarzenegger backed Proposition 187 and won handily as governor. Cruz Bustamante won just over 50 percent of the Hispanic vote and was against it."

"Yeah, but when you add the Hispanic votes for Michael Camejo, the state's Green Party candidate, to Bustamante's votes, the Republicans still didn't come close." John responded.

"You're right," Lee confessed. "The California Hispanic vote remains solidly Democratic and liberal, but they are not the voters that get out the vote in large numbers. Proposition 187 would win again. Taking a firm stand that is measured and balanced can't be too poisonous. People are frustrated. I think they are looking for people with some solutions we can start working with. Besides, with a popular President trying to find his way on this, I think something is going to be done."

"Bush can't do it alone," John said.

"Some Republican, including Rep. Jim Kolbe of Arizona and Sen. Larry Craig of Idaho, criticized Bush for not including in his plan a guaranteed way to get permanent residency without leaving the country" Lee added. "Not all Republicans are against earned citizenship."

"They are a minority in the party, and you know it," Kelly said.

"That may be true, but whatever we decide tonight, Bush's Hispanic record will help him on Tuesday," Lee said. "Bush got one third of the Hispanic vote in 2000 compared to Bob Dole's 21%. With the positions he has taken, he hopes to reach 50% next week against Kerry. That will get him four more years to work on this. And if he picks up seats in Congress, as hoped, that will be even better."

"I hope you are right," John said. "I think your measured view has some merit. I hope there are people fighting hard to develop a workable plan."

"I think there is a lot of work behind the scenes trying to find the right path," Lee said. "I think they will find it because people are frustrated and the time may be right. Failure to act soon will just make it worse. And at the same time, we have to remember where we started. We have to support the *Mexican Dream* and to honor the great Americans of Hispanic descent who've made and continue to make such a valued contribution to our country."

"I hope no American forgets that," John said. "Or the value of all those great Swedes."

"Of course," Lee said with a smile.

"Dear, I think it is time to go home before Lee comes up with any more issues," Lynn said. "We *all* have church tomorrow morning."

"We wouldn't want to get any of us in trouble with God," Kelly replied. "Besides, after church, Lee and I finish walking our precinct for Republican Women Federated."

"I *now* know how committed Republican women are to *walking their talk*, but here's the big question," John said. "We all go to church. Is God Republican or Democrat?"

"Republican," Lee said quickly. "It's says so clearly in the Bible."

"Where?" Lynn asked.

"Ecclesiastes 10:2-3," Lee said. "The heart of the wise inclines to the right, the heart of the fool to the left. And even as he walks down the road, the fool lacks sense and shows everyone how stupid he is."

"You're kidding?" John said laughing. "It says that?"

"It does," Lee said firmly.

"That has nothing to do with being a Republican or a Democrat!" Lynn said defiantly.

"You are *absolutely* right," Lee confessed. "I just wanted to get one more rise out of you two to get you awake for the drive home. Look, there are an ample number of good Christians on both sides of this divide."

"Thank goodness you said that," Lynn agreed.

"Seriously, I think Christians may make a difference in this year's election," Lee responded.

"What do you mean?" John asked.

"The popularity and impact of Mel Gibson's *The Passion of the Christ* is one reason," Lee said. "Do you remember the young man in Kansas who confessed to killing his girlfriend after seeing the movie and talking to his pastor?"

"Of course," Lynn said. "I remember reading about that."

"This film continues to set all kinds of records, and it's impacting people's lives," Lee continued.

"What does that have to do with the election?" Lynn asked.

"In 2000, just 50% of Christian conservatives even voted," Lee answered. "If even 58% vote there could be a landside. Some have said we are now in a culture war. I wouldn't go that far. But I think many Christians are not going to stay on the sidelines this election."

"Not all Christians are Bush supporters," John countered.

"I agree," Lee said. "I think we sometimes get carried away about telling others what God thinks we ought to do politically. Jesus didn't come to change governments in Rome or Jerusalem. He came to change people's lives. I try to remember the comments by C.S. Lewis, 'He who converts his neighbor has performed the most practical Christian-political act of all.' I think we in the church ought to put more of an emphasis on sharing the Gospel and not use the pulpit to tell people how to vote."

"I agree," Lynn said. "That sounds like another dinner conversation worth having, but not tonight!"

"Agreed! After all, there are good religious people of all faiths on both sides of this political divide," Lee said. "I just hope after this conversation there is a chance we can pull *you* over to our side on this election."

"The movies I love best have a happy ending," John said. "But this is not a movie. This is an election that requires a lot of deliberation. I must confess that before today, I was not planning on voting for Bush. I will consider that now. That's a step for this life-long Democrat."

"I'm not sure I will," Lynn said. "I may e-mail you a couple of questions before Tuesday's vote. I want to think about this a lot more after I have had some sleep. Hint, hint! John, it's time we go."

"Good idea. Both Kelly and I would be glad to respond to any questions you have," Lee said. "We may not have all the answers, but we can get you to someone who does."

"All this politics aside," Kelly added. "I loved meeting you both. Lee talked about John, and now I know why he was so excited about getting together. We must do it again."

"Next time," John said. "We bring you to the Democratic side of town. And I think we may have to bring reinforcements if we decide to take this conversation any further."

"Hey, if it was as fun as this conversation," Lee said. "The more the merrier."

"Drive safely now," Kelly added. "Here's hoping we'll talk again soon."

"We'll call you after the election," John said. "I may even tell you how I voted."

Epilogue

*"I guess the truth can hurt you worse in an
election than about anything that could
happen to you." –Will Rogers*

One of the reasons I wrote this book as a dialogue between informed citizens is because the right to dialogue may very well be the beginning of freedom, but it is the necessity of listening and reacting that makes that right important. In far too many political communications people do not listen. In some cases *political experts* seem to provide more confusion than clarity. In other communication forums, strong statements may rally the faithful, but, unfortunately, such partisan messages turn others off before they even begin to understand what is being said.

This is not a position paper drafted by the Republican Party. It is one Republican couple's thoughts about why they vote as they do. People vote for different reasons; they have different ideas about how to put their party's principles into action. That is part of what makes America so special. . .and so free.

I confess that from a political perspective this book is one-sided. John and Lynn asked Lee and Kelly to help them understand why they chose to be Republicans. It was not a debate, but rather a journey to understand and to react to what they learned. I tried to honestly convey comments that John and Lynn might have had; you will have to judge whether I was fair in reflecting their Democratic positions and concerns. It is hard to claim the liberty of free expression unless you're willing to give it to others. I would eagerly read a similar dinner dialogue explaining Democratic principles.

"A fanatic is someone who can't change his mind and won't change the subject." –Winston Churchill

195

There are many facts used in this book. As with any conversation, they are important in making points, but such *facts* provide snapshots of political reality for one moment in time. Such data points change over time, but the principles discussed tend to be more lasting. That is why the emphasis of this book was on guiding principles.

The dialogue is over, but the book is not finished. I challenge you to take *The Thinking Voter's Guide* that follows. I trust it will help you sort out what *you believe* on the principles and values that separate Republicans and Democrats in America today. You may be surprised at how you score.

I trust this book will start your own dinner dialogues about why you vote the way you do. Never be afraid to give a reason for the positions that you hold but work to express your positions with gentleness and respect. Care enough to also seek to understand the positions of others.

And when the dialogue is over, don't forget to exercise the right you have as an American citizen to vote. Liberty is not a one time thing. Liberty must be earned and reearned by every age in every single election. Exercise your hard earned privilege—Vote! Even better—Vote Republican!

America's future is not guaranteed...

Sir Alex Fraser Tytler, noted Scottish jurist and historian, wrote over 200 years ago on the fall of the Athenian Republic:

> "A democracy cannot exist as a permanent form of government. It can only exist until the voters discover that they can vote themselves largesse from the public treasury. From that moment on the majority always votes for the candidates promising the most benefits from the public treasury, with the result that a democracy always collapses over a loose fiscal policy, always followed by a dictatorship. The average age of the world's greatest civilizations has been two hundred years. These nations have progressed through this sequence: from bondage to spiritual faith; from spiritual faith to great courage; from courage to liberty; from liberty to abundance; from abundance to selfishness; from selfishness to complacency; from complacency to apathy; from apathy to dependence; from dependency back again into bondage."

May we continue to prove him wrong...

A Thinking Voter's Guide

Compiled By Terry Paulson, PhD

Make a Thoughtful Decision when You Vote:

None of the short political commercials from either political party do justice to the issues we face as a state or country. The media and political ads often seem preoccupied with negatives and provocative sound bytes. After reading *The Dinner*, this guide is designed to help you think through your voting decision on the basis of issues that are important to you. The twenty issues identified will help isolate the voting tendencies of the Republican and Democratic parties. It is our collective responsibility to make thoughtful choices in any election. I hope this guide helps you do that. It is expansive enough to help you identify most of the critical issues of the day that ought to be considered. The test scoring also allows you to individualize the test to give more weight to the issues that are most important to you in making your vote.

The Truth Is in the Tension Between the Parties:

I hope you agree that most of the citizens on both sides of our political divide care about our country. There are extreme members of both parties who are embarrassments to members in their respective groups. While both parties care about the future of this country, there are major differences as to the best way to achieve that future. In each issue isolated, I have tried to identify the general tendency of each party in as unemotional and specific way as I can. On each issue, check the party that most reflects your opinion. It is rare that you will support any one party on all issues, so try to be honest with yourself in scoring each issue.

Individualize Your Issue Weighting:

As with any decision, you bring a unique set of priorities to your choice of how to vote. In each of the twenty issues, you will be asked to identify the position you most identify with. Totaling your Democrat and Republican position votes should help you determine your vote selection in November.

Certainly, some issues are more important to you than others in any given election. In addition, some issues are not important to you at all. To adjust for that difference in an issue's level of importance, at the end of the test you can increase the weight of your *most important issue* to **three points**. You can increase the weight of up to *three additional important issues* by giving those issues an increased weighting of **two points**. To account for the fact that some issues are not important to you at all, you can **cross off up to three issues** to discount their significance in making your decision. *Wait to the end after reviewing all issues to make those decisions and then add up your total vote preference scores.*

Now the Issues that Count...

1. Government Size and Intervention:

___ **Democrat:** While wanting to curtail waste, fraud and abuse, government intervention is still critical in meeting the needs of our complex society. The obstacles faced by some American individuals and businesses today are too difficult for them to face on their own; the federal and state governments must remain active in developing programs and funding agencies to meet those expanding needs.

___ **Republican:** Government should be limited to critical roles that people cannot do for themselves. Politicians should work to keep more money in the pockets of American citizens by reducing the size and scope of government by ending unnecessary programs and avoiding starting new ones. Work to keep the power and resources close to the people though their local governments rather than through a centralized and distant state or federal government.

2. Government Regulations:

___ **Democrat:** One of the principle functions of government should be to regulate and control the actions and performance of corporations, organizations and individuals who can impact the environment, health, or safety of our citizens. The rules, forms and controls generated are a cost that businesses and individuals are obligated to fulfill to protect citizens and the environment.

___ **Republican:** We support the free-enterprise system with minimal controls as a positive force for creating economic growth, more jobs, and personal wealth for its citizens. Government regulations and controls are necessary but should be limited to high-priority concerns. The emphasis should be on enforcing accountability for the rules and controls that are in force. Extensive regulations and paperwork increase costs, make it hard for businesses to compete, and make states less attractive for needed business investment.

3. Social Services or Self-Reliance:

___ **Democrat:** Welfare reform, while necessary, has gone too far in cutting back services for the truly needy. True caring is expressed in government programs that can allocate more resources for people unable to cope with the demands of our society. As a wealthy, industrialized society, our government should be more involved in providing funds and programs that insure the health and happiness of the less fortunate. Private charity cannot meet the needs without strong government involvement and funds. Self-reliance is not for everyone; it takes a village.

___ **Republican:** Measure true caring by how many people no longer need government programs and are self-sufficient instead of by how many are served by welfare aid. We have made progress in getting people off welfare and back into living productive lives. We must continue to care enough to keep a safety net that assists those in need without allowing the net to become a dependency trap for those who are capable of working. Private charity is more efficient and can be more effective when coupled with some government support. Self-reliance in support of the American Dream is a critical American value that must be supported with tough love.

4. Crime Policy:

___ **Democrat:** Because of the unfair application of the justice system, strong discretion is needed for judges to establish fair sentencing. Punishment should be applied, but rehabilitation should be as important as punishment. Capital punishment should be minimized if not stopped. Controls on the police must be established to insure fair treatment of all, an end to racial profiling, and strong punishment for hate crimes. More money should be spent on programs to prevent crime than on constructing more prisons.

___ **Republican:** Because of the tendency of the legal system to err on the side of leniency, strong guidelines such as "the Three Strikes Law" should remain in place to insure accountability and punishment for crimes. Capital punishment should be rare but should be considered in first-degree murder cases. Accountability over rehabilitation should be stressed. The rights of the victims should be more important than protecting criminals. An investment in adequate prisons and police is a wise investment.

5. Tort Reforms:

___ **Democrat:** The rights of individuals and groups to sue in order to right wrongs must be expanded beyond the current limits. By increasing pain and suffering judgments, judges and juries will be able to send a strong message to irresponsible companies that unethical and illegal behavior will not be tolerated. To require the loser to pay legal costs or to limit judgments is to tip the scales in the favor of the rich and corporations at the expense of those who are least able to defend themselves.

___ **Republican:** Individuals and groups should have the right to sue, but the growing use of frivolous lawsuits is costing all Americans and is making a lottery out of our courts. "Victim thinking" has been taken to an extreme and pain and suffering limits must be maintained. "Loser pay" provisions, limits on *pain and suffering* judgments and limits on the share of judgments going to lawyers should be considered in future tort reforms.

6. Education Policy:

___ **Democrat:** We need to invest more money into our classrooms. We should be funding additional teachers and giving our public schools the funds they need to improve the educational excellence of our youth. Charter schools and standard testing will help achieve this. A separation of church and state must be maintained in our schools. Only those able to afford private schools should be able to use them. Home schooling should have more controls to insure the quality of instruction.

___ **Republican:** We are committed to educational excellence in support of the goal of leaving no child behind. Our public education system is not producing results. Our youth "feel" more competent but consistently perform at low levels of achievement compared to other industrial countries. A strong education system that works is very important to the future of our country. We must give more control to local schools, give vouchers a chance to prove themselves where states want to experiment, and support home schooling and more parent choice where possible.

7. Tax Policy:

___ **Democrat:** Fairness must take into account that those who are able to pay should pay significantly more than others. Because of the rewards our society affords the successful achievers, they should be expected to shoulder more of the costs to sustain the government that maintains that opportunity. To make a flatter system or provide an across-the-board tax cut for all levels would unfairly benefit primarily the rich. Because of the wealth of the rich citizens, it is not unfair to have 10% of American workers paying 60% of the income tax bill. Surpluses should be used to pay down the debt and help fund new, needed programs.

___ **Republican:** No matter what form tax relief or reforms take, Republicans support minimizing taxes to the lowest appropriate level possible in order to maintain work incentives in support of the American Dream, minimize unnecessary government growth and waste, and stimulate the dynamic growth of our economy. During difficult economic times tax cuts stimulate the economy and the business growth that keeps economies growing. Where possible, tax rates should be flatter and tax regulations simpler. All but the poorest Americans should pay some of the load.

8. Military Support and Homeland Security:

___ **Democrat:** While a strong military and a secure homeland are both important, we must put an even stronger emphasis on diplomacy, restraint and U.N. cooperation. The best defense is expanded commerce with shared technology and mutual interests. Democrats state that they want to sustain a strong military, but they do not want to let increased investment in military expenditures curtail the government from funding needed homeland security, domestic programs and social services.

___ Republican: In a world with more rogue countries and terrorist groups capable of attacking our homeland, America must invest adequate resource to remain strong, progressive, and technologically sophisticated. We must continue to walk softly but continue to carry a big, technologically-advanced stick that is positioned to deal with new, smaller engagements wherever necessary. The new realities in a free world open to terrorism, make investing in homeland security and our military a necessary and expensive priority we must fund to stay safe.

9. What Special Interests Do You Most Support:

___ Democrat: The primary sources of special interest funding for campaigns remain the trial lawyers, the NEA (the teachers union), the entertainment industry, and unions in general. Aligning yourself with these groups' values concerns you less, and you fear the influence of the Republican special interest groups more.

___ Republican: The primary sources of special interest funding for campaigns remain large business, small business, conservative Christian groups, and the NRA (National Rifle Association). Aligning yourself with these groups' values concerns you less, and you fear the influence of the Democratic special interest groups more.

10. The Environment:

___ Democrat: Strong action is needed now to protect future generations from the effects of unchecked business interests and global warming. Limitations now are a small price to pay for a future for our children and endangered species. The scientific data is conclusive enough to warrant new regulations and limitations on American businesses and oil exploration. Put a bigger investment into alternative energy.

___ Republican: There is no consistent evidence of global warming any more than there was evidence of the global cooling and the ice age predicted in the 70s. We must be good stewards of the environment without making radical unsubstantiated interventions. Extreme regulations and environmental limits make us less competitive globally and lose jobs. Work to expand domestic energy sources, oil and alternative energy to decrease foreign dependence.

11. Separation of Church and State:

___ **Democrat:** The separation of church and state is a firm value that must be maintained at all levels of government. There should be less display of religious conviction or holidays of any sort in schools or on government property. Personal faith is important but should be separated from any kind of public support. No government or voucher funds should be used in any religious school.

___ **Republican:** We must support the value of religious faith as a cornerstone for the values and moral compass that helps sustain our country. We must not institutionalize any one religion, but we must insure that freedom "of" religion should never become freedom "from" religion. Separation of church and state is not meant to limit reference to God or to stop the free exercise of religious faith by a minority or a majority believer. Vouchers and public support for proven religious service programs should be allowed.

12. Affirmative Action:

___ **Democrat:** Societal bias and wrongs still exist to the extent that additional support for racial minorities is warranted. Race preference regulations should be sustained to make sure that more minorities are hired and more minority students are selected by college programs.

___ **Republican:** While still rigorously defending civil rights laws, we must work to create a color-blind society that puts an end to quota preference systems on the basis of race. Race ought to be irrelevant. Affirmative action needs to be reframed to allow support of any citizen on the basis of need, not race.

13. Hate Crime Legislation:

___ **Democrat:** To insure the protection of rights for minority groups, some crimes, attacks and murders against minority group members are so heinous that the federal government should be allowed to intervene to insure prosecution. A hateful murder or crime against a minority member is dangerous to our society's values and warrants additional punishment.

___ **Republican:** To single out crimes against any one minority group for increased prosecution is not wise. Equal protection under the law is an important value that must be maintained. Rather than single out "hate" crimes, we should work to insure that all crimes are punished strongly. Adequate laws exist; the will to punish strongly must be maintained.

14. Gay Rights:

___ **Democrat:** Because gays are an abused minority in America, we should work to provide civil rights protection and equal status for same-sex marriages including the right to adopt children. Efforts should be made to develop and promote early-childhood interventions that promote tolerance and acceptance of gay relationships and lifestyles.

___ **Republican:** Gay citizens should be afforded equal protection under the law but deserve no special civil rights protection. No special training should be provided in the schools that promotes acceptance of a gay lifestyle; tolerance should not require agreement. A Constitutional Amendment affirming marriage as a union between a man and a woman should be passed. Civil unions between gay citizens should be a state-rights issue.

15. Social Security Reforms:

___ **Democrat:** Democrats have taken a stand for applying any budget surpluses to help deal with the Social Security Fund shortfalls but have proposed no changes in the plan with any long range implications. They have rejected bipartisan task-force suggestions to consider investment funds, lower cost-of-living calculations, and any change in support. A lockbox of funds is proposed. A proposal to allow additional funds to be invested to enhance Social Security payments is proposed.

____ **Republican:** Although viable at this time, our Social Security Fund is in serious long-term trouble. When baby boomers retire, working Americans will be facing higher payroll taxes unless changes occur. New proposals call for a lockbox of funds and allowing a small percentage of payroll taxes to be used by citizens to invest in their own investment options while still meeting the obligations to those already retired.

16. Immigration Controls:

____ **Democrat:** The tradition of America is strongly supportive of being a welcoming country for immigrants. Any limitations to illegal immigration should be limited to making entry difficult. Once here and contributing, even illegal aliens should be allowed to find their rightful place in our society and open to receiving the benefits of citizenship. Bilingual education should be provided to assist large immigrant groups.

____ **Republican:** The tradition of America is strongly supportive of being a welcoming country for immigrants. Those who arrive here legally must be supported and embraced as part of the rich American mosaic. It is proposed that illegal immigrants who have jobs should be required to register as guest workers with the eventual return to their country of origin. English-first education focus should be used to help all immigrants learn our language as quickly as possible.

17. Minimum Wage:

____ **Democrat:** The great American economy is not getting the rewards down to the poor working Americans. We need to increase the minimum wage to a higher level to allow the poorest Americans to benefit from our economy. The gap between the *have's* and the *have-not's* must be addressed through government policy and intervention.

____ **Republican:** Increasing the minimum wage while providing short-term reward for those whose bosses can afford to pay it, will also cause some companies to go under and some workers to lose jobs. Most minimum wage employees do not stay in that job. They can use entry-level jobs to prove their worth, learn new skills, and then move to jobs that pay more. Getting beyond minimum wage jobs is one incentive to keep improving and learning.

18. Healthcare Reform:

___ **Democrat:** There are too many Americans who are falling through the cracks in healthcare coverage. More should be done to pass a patient bill of rights that addresses the inadequacies of healthcare coverage. Medicare coverage should be extended to more citizens who have no healthcare coverage. The efficiencies of scale and the scope of the problem warrant federal remedies and we should work towards universal coverage, starting first by covering all children.

___ **Republican:** Any form of socialized medicine should be resisted or at least minimized to those with the greatest need. The expanded drug benefit for seniors should mix competition and personal accountability with government support. It is best to let competition keep viable healthcare options for Americans to choose from. Tax-free Medical Savings accounts and major-medical plans should be used to allow citizens to get better control of their healthcare costs.

19. Abortion:

___ **Democrat:** Sustain our current abortion policy that emphasizes the woman's right to choose an abortion with minimal restrictions. We should be proud of the fact that in industrialized countries, only Japan has a more unrestricted abortion policy than the United States. Serious limits should be placed on Pro-Life demonstrations close to abortion clinics. The banning of late-term abortions is a step in the wrong direction.

___ **Republican:** Although Republicans vary strongly, most agree with the need to establish limits on abortion to make them rare. A fetus may not be a baby, but it is more than a mass of tissue. We support the ban on late-term, partial-birth abortions and should work to establish parental notification. Pro-Life demonstrators should be allowed the same rights of expression any other American is allowed.

20. Gun Control:

___ **Democrat:** Continue to make it more difficult for citizens to buy guns by retail and at gun shows without adequate checks or delays. Increase the pressure to ban the sale of automatic and semi-automatic weapons. Hold gun manufacturers responsible for increasing the safety of guns. Pass more laws restricting gun purchase and possession.

___ **Republican:** Resist any major change in gun laws beyond more efficient and immediate checking for criminal records. The right to bear arms is a Constitutional right that should be protected. Guns don't kill people; people kill people. Support gun safety and strong penalties for criminal use. Enforce existing laws restricting gun purchase and possession.

Determining
Your Voting Score

Make one issue your top priority and score that issue **3 points.**
Make up to three others important by scoring them **2 points each.**
Cross off up to three issues because they are not important to you. **Do not count them.**
Give **1 point** to each remaining issue.

Add Up Party Points:

Democratic Issue Points: ____

Republican Issue Points: ____

Voting Team or Individuals: In most cases discerning American citizens learn to vote for any candidate from the political team that most effectively stands for the principles, values, and positions that best matches their own views. A winning President will use his/her Rolodex to appoint skilled and like-minded politicians and the judges, leaders, and professionals he or she will appoint to key positions. In Congress, the party in power has committee control to increase their influence. But in a given race, the personal, ethical and/or illegal actions of a given candidate can so concern you that you will choose in isolated situations to vote against your voting tendencies.

Now VOTE! This country is not run by polls but by the voters that show up!

About Your Author

Terry L. Paulson, PhD
www.unitedwecanwin.com
www.terrypaulson.com
Paulson and Associates Inc.
Agoura Hills, CA

Dr. Terry Paulson is a PhD psychologist, an author and honored professional speaker. He was selected to the National Speakers Association's prestigious *CPAE Speaker Hall of Fame* along with Norman Vincent Peale, Ronald Reagan and Colin Powell.

For over 30 years, Dr. Paulson has helped organizations, leaders, and teams make change work. He has developed positive approaches and practical techniques that have made him in demand as a speaker all over the world for *Fortune 500* companies, mid-size companies, hospitals, government agencies and associations. *Meeting News* picked him as a "Best Bet" speaker. The *LA Times* said he was a speaker with "substance and style." *Business Digest* called him the "Will Rogers of management consultants." He brings knowledge, enthusiasm and a unique and tasteful sense of humor to every speech he gives and every book he writes. No complicated theories, just straight talk laced with targeted, real-life strategies and stories entertainingly presented to get his message across.

Dr. Paulson is a long-time Republican who has spoken to numerous Republican groups. His political comments have been shared in *USA Today*, the *Los Angeles Times*, and the *Wall Street Journal*. He currently writes a monthly opinion column for the *Ventura County Star.*

Share *The Dinner...*

Bulk Discounts: Discounts on *The Dinner* start at only 10 copies. Save up to 50% off retail price for large orders.

Custom Publishing: Private label a cover with your organization's name and logo. Or, tailor information to your needs with a custom insert that personalizes your copies.

Support Information: Visit www.unitedwecanwin.com to find other op-ed columns and articles by Dr. Paulson. You may also want to register for his regular e-Zine, *United We Can Win.*

Dynamic Speaker: Dr. Paulson travels internationally presenting programs on leadership and making change work. He is available to speak to your company or organization with topics that energize, inform and entertain.

Contact Paulson and Associates Inc.

**Call now at 1-818-991-5110 or e-mail me at
info@unitedwecanwin.com
www.terrypaulson.com**

**Amber Eagle Press
Paulson and Associates Inc.
P. O. Box 365
Agoura Hills, CA 91376-0365
www.unitedwecanwin.com**

Books Worth Reading...

Coulter, Ann. *Slander: Liberal Lies about the American Right*, Crown Publishers, NY, NY, 2002.

D'Souza, Dinesh. *Ronald Reagan: How an Ordinary Man Became an Extraordinary Leader*, Free Press, NY, NY, 1997.

Elder, Larry. *The Ten Things You Can't Say in America*, St. Martin's Press, NY, NY, 2000.

Elder, Larry. *Showdown,* St. Martin's Press, NY, NY, 2004.

Friedman, Milton. *Capitalism and Freedom*, University of Chicago Press, Chicago, 1982.

Geisler, Norman and Turek, Frank. *Legislating Morality*, Bethany House Publishers, Minneapolis, MN, 1998.

Goldberg, Bernard. *Arrogance: Rescuing America From the Media Elite,* Warner Books, NY, NY, 2003.

Hannity, Sean. *Deliver Us from Evil*, Regan Books, NY, NY, 2004.

Hayek, F.A. *The Road to Serfdom*, University of Chicago Press, Chicago, 1994.

Ingraham, Laura. *Shut Up and Sing: How Elites from Hollywood, Politics, and the UN are Subverting America*, Regnery Publishing, NY, NY, 2003.

Lomborg, Bjørn. *The Skeptical Environmentalist*, Cambridge University Press, Cambridge, 2001.

Limbaugh, Rush. *The Way Things Ought to Be*, Pocket Books, NY, NY, 1992.

McInerney, Thomas and Vallely, Paul. *Endgame: The Blueprint for Victory in the War on Terror*, Regnery Publishing, 2004.

Miller, Zen. *A National Party No More: The Conscience of a Conservative Democrat*, Stroud & Hall, NY, NY, 2003.

Noonan, Peggy. *When Character Was King: A Story of Ronald Reagan*, Viking, NY, NY, 2001.

O'Reilly, Bill. *The O'Reilly Factor*, Broadway Books, NY, NY, 2000.

O'Reilly, Bill. *The No Spin Zone*, Broadway Books, NY, NY, 2001.

Parker, Star. *Uncle Sam's Plantation*, WND Books, Nashville, TN, 2003.

Prager, Dennis. *Happiness Is a Serious Problem: A Human Nature Repair Manual,*, Regan Books, NY, NY, 1998.

Prager, Dennis. *Think a Second Time*, Regan Books, NY, NY, 1995.

Sowell, Thomas. *Basic Economics: A Citizen's Guide to the Economy*, Basic Books, NY, NY, 2004.

Stossel, John. *Give Me a Break*, Harper Collins, NY, NY, 2004.

Sykes, Charles J. *A Nation of Victims: The Decay of the American Character*, St. Martin's Press, NY, NY, 1992.

Thompson, Carolyn and Ware, James. *The Leadership Genius of George W. Bush*, John Wiley & Sons, New Jersey, 2003.

Other Books by Dr. Paulson...

Paulson, Terry. *They Shoot Managers Don't They?* Ten Speed Press, Berkeley, CA, 1991.

Paulson, Terry. *Making Humor Work,* Crisp Publications, Inc., Menlo Park, CA, 1989.

Paulson, Terry. *Paulson on Change*, Griffin Publishing, Glendale, CA, 1995.

Paulson, Terry. *50 Tips for Speaking Like a Pro*, Crisp Publications, Menlo Park, CA, 1999.

Paulson, Terry and Paulson, Sean. *Can I Have the Keys to the Car?* Augsburg Fortress, Minneapolis, MN, 1999.

Sanborn, Mark and Paulson, Terry. *Meditations for the Road Warrior*, Baker Books, Grand Rapids, MI, 1998.

References

CHAPTER ONE

Sources: Ronald Reagan remarks at Ford Claycomo Assembly Plant, Kansas City, Missouri, 1984, in 2001 Calendar from the Ronald Reagan Presidential Foundation, 40 Presidential Dr., Simi Valley, CA 93065; Groucho Marx, in Bob Ross, *The Laugh Connection*, Spring 1993.

CHAPTER TWO

Sources: Abraham Lincoln, quoted by John Wooden, in Cal Fussman, "Coach!" *UCLA Magazine*, Summer 2000, pp. 22-27; Will Rogers, compiled by Joe Richard Dunn, PhD, "The JRD Collection of Humor Quotes," Jackson, MS, *Humor and Health Institute*, 1995, p. 14.

CHAPTER THREE

Sources: Winston Churchill, in *Religion and Liberty*, November and December, 2001, back cover, p. 16; Ronald Reagan, in Tony Snow, "The Wisdom and Humor of Ronald Reagan," Creators Syndicate, 1995; Marvin Zonis, University of Chicago, in presentation to *KPMG Consumer Markets Audit Executives Forum*, April 17-18, 2001, Santa Barbara, CA.

CHAPTER FOUR

Sources: W. Michael Cox and Richard Alm, "By Our Own Bootstraps," Federal Reserve Bank of Dallas, 214-922-5189.

CHAPTER FIVE

Sources: Martin Luther King, Jr., in Peter Brimelow and Leslie Spencer, "When Quotas Replace Merit, Everybody Suffers," *Forbes*, February 15, 1993, pp. 80-102; Booker T. Washington, quoted in Michael F. Dulles, "Neo Slavery vs. Classical Slavery;" Steven Roberts, "Lift Every Voice and Sing a New Song," *US News and World Report*, April 19, 1993, p. 8; Ward Connerly, "Affirmative Action Has Outlived Its Usefulness," *Black Enterprise*, November 1995, p. 157; Niki Butler Mitchell, *The New Color of Success: 20 Young Black Millionaires Tell You How They're Making It*, Prima Publishing, 2000, in *USA Today*, February 28, 2000, B-6; John McWhorter, *Losing the Race: Self-Sabotage in Black America;* Larry Elder, *Ten Things You Can't Say in America;* David Horowitz, *The Death of the Civil Rights Movement;* Jeffrey Hart, "Jesse Jackson, Please Go Away," King Features Syndicate, *Conservative Chronicle*, March 7, 2001, p. 25; Jeffrey Hart, "Jesse Jackson's Money Machine," King Features Syndicate, *Conservative Chronicle*, April 18, 2001, p. 5; Thomas Sowell, "Affirmative Action Fraud:

Part III," Creators Syndicate, *Conservative Chronicle*, April 16, 2003, p. 6;
Thomas Sowell, "Affirmative Action Fraud: Part I," Creators Syndicate,
Conservative Chronicle, April 9, 2003, p. 25; Patricia Raybon, *Newsweek*,
October 2, 1989, p. 11.

CHAPTER SIX

Sources: Condoleezza Rice, in Rush Limbaugh, *The Limbaugh Letter*,
August 1999, p. 9; Marlene Adler Marks, "Outside the Ethnic Box," *LA
Times Magazine*, February 20, 2000, pp. 14-17, 36; Richard Florida, "Gay-
tolerant Communities Prosper," *USA Today*, May 1, 2003; Pepperdine
University's Institute for Public Policy Study, "The Emerging Latino Middle
Class," *The Ventura Count Star*, November 10, 1996, D-8; Chris Gardner
Segment, ABC's *20/20*, January 17, 2003; Jim Hopkins, "Female Owned
Companies Flourish," *USA Today*, May 6, 2003, B-1; Thomas Sowell,
"Affirmative Action Fraud: Part II," Creators Syndicate, *Conservative
Chronicle*, April 9, 2003, p. 29.

CHAPTER SEVEN

Sources: Ronald Reagan, *Simpson's Contemporary Quotations*, compiled by
James B. Simpson, 1988, quote #2870, , "On the Campaign Trail," *NY Times*,
Sept. 22, 1980; Ronald Reagan, in Lou Cannon, "The Role of a Lifetime,"
July 2, 1991, p. 812; Naomi Wolf, *New Republic,* in John Leo, "Abortion
Brutality Goes beyond Rights Debate," Universal Press Syndicate, 1995; "A
Gallup Poll Determined 70 Percent Back a Law to Bar It," a January 10-12
CNN/USA Today/Gallup poll, in Media Research Center CyberAlert, January
30, 2003, Vol. Eight, No. 19; Partial birth position of AMA and C. Everett
Koop, in Sean Hannity, *Let Freedom Ring*, Regan Books/Harper Collins,
2002, p. 182; "Abortions Per 1,000 Women: Maryland: 29 Pennsylvania:
14.3," Linda Douglass, *ABC News*, Washington, in Media Research Center
CyberAlert, January 23, 2003, Vol. Eight, No. 14; Stephen Chapman, "The
Fictitious Threat to Abortion Rights," Creators Syndicate Inc., *Conservative
Chronicles*, April 23, 2003, p. 10; Kisher & Irving, "The Human Develop-
ment Hoax: Time to Tell the Truth," *Gold Leaf Press*, 1997, pp. 7-10; Rita
Ruben, "Survey Finds U.S. Abortion Rate Hits Lowest Level since 1974,"
USA Today, January 12, 2000; John Ankerberg and John Weldon, *When Does
Life Begin?* Brentwood, Tennessee, Woglemuth and Hyatt, Publishers, 1989;
California Medicine, Vol. 113, No. 3, September, 1970; Landrum B. Shettles,
Rites of Life: The Scientific Evidence for Life Before Birth, Grand Rapids,
Michigan, Zondervan, 1983; Subcommittee on Separation of Powers, *Report
to Senate Judiciary Committee* S-158, 97th Congress, 1st Session, 1981;
Ronald Reagan, *Abortion and the Conscience of the Nation*, Nashville,
Tennessee, Thomas Nelson Publishers, 1984; Jesse Helms, *When Free Men
Shall Stand*, Grand Rapids, Michigan, Zondervan, 1976; Jerry Falwell, *Listen*

America! Garden City, New York, Doubleday & Company, 1980; Professor Glendon, "Abortion and Divorce in American Law," in Dennis Prager, "Abortion: The Case for Compromise," March 5, 1991, lecture on tape, www.dennisprager.com/.

CHAPTER EIGHT

Sources: Peter Drucker, *Wired*, March, 1998, p. 161; Booker T. Washington, *Forbes*, Dec. 5, 1994, p. 87; William Bennett, "The Crisis in American Education," *World Affairs Journal*, September 17, 1993, pp. 97-103; Stephen Goldsmith, Mayor of Indianapolis, *Forbes*, September 23, 1996, p. 32; John Taylor Gatto, 1991 New York State Teacher of the Year, in Rush Limbaugh, *See I Told You So*, Pocket Books, 1993, p. 187; Rush Limbaugh, *The Limbaugh Letter*, March, 1997, p. 3; Paul E. Peterson, *Forbes*, Nov. 3, 1997, p. 32; David Boaz, *Liberating Schools;* John Wooden, quotes compiled by Joe Richard Dunn, PhD, "The JRD Collection of Humor Quotes," Jackson, MS, *Humor and Health Institute*, 1995, p. 16.

CHAPTER NINE

Sources: Peter Drucker, *LA Times*, March 2, 1997, M-3; Thomas Jefferson's First Inaugural, *The Claremont Institute—Precepts*, http://www.claremont.org, No. 226, May 17, 2000; Ben Franklin, in Rush Limbaugh, "Monster Government," *Limbaugh Letter*, August, 2001 p. 3; Albert Einstein, in Rush Limbaugh, *See I Told You So*, Pocket Books, 1993, p. 252; Jeff Jacoby, "The Republican Party's Spending Orgy," *Conservative Chronicle*, July 30, 2003, p. 17; Governor Arnold Schwarzenegger, in Rush Limbaugh, "The Rush Profile: Gov. Arnold Schwarzenegger," *Limbaugh Letter*, February, 2004, p. 6; Everett Dirksen, "History Lesson," *Business 2.0*, June 12, 2001, p. 5; John Stossel, *Give Me a Break*, Harper Collins, 2003, pp. 131-132; *National Academy of Sciences Report*, in Jeff Jacoby, *Boston Globe,* in Rush Limbaugh, "SUVs and Freedom," *Limbaugh Letter*, August, 2001, p. 8; T.J. Rogers, CEO of Cypress Semi-conductor, *Cato Institute* tape, April, 2000.

CHAPTER TEN

Sources: George Bernard Shaw, in *Speaker's Idea File*, Ragan Communications, 212 W. Superior St., #200, Chicago, IL 60610, 312-335-0037, 1-800-878-5331, promotional brochure sample, p. 15; Ronald Reagan, display at Reagan Presidential Library, March, 1997; John F. Kennedy, to The Economic Club of New York, December 4, 1962, in Rush Limbaugh, "My Conversation with John F. Kennedy," *The Limbaugh Letter*, August, 1993; George W. Bush, in *Conservative Chronicle*, March 22, 2000, p. 6; John Adams, in Rush Limbaugh, *See I Told You So*, Pocket Books, 1993, p. 280; Michael Medved, 870 AM—KRLA Radio broadcast, April 15, 2004; Stephen Moore, President of Club for Growth, in Rush Limbaugh, *Limbaugh*

Letter, April, 2001, p. 10; Walter Williams, Creators Syndicate Inc., 1995; Bob Novak, in interview with Stephen Moore, President of Club for Growth, in Rush Limbaugh, *Limbaugh Letter*, April, 2001, p. 10; Humorous Tax Form, *US News and World Report*, January 8, 1990, p. 68.

CHAPTER ELEVEN

Sources: Martha Farnsworth Riche, President of Farnsworth Riche Associates, "Best of the Best," *Fast Company*, June, 2001, pp. 82-102; Dinesh D'Souza, "Lottery of Success," *Business 2.0*, December 12, 2000, pp. 218-235; Peter Drucker, *Forbes*, March 10, 1997, p. 124; Donald Lambro, "Media Short Bush's Investment Plan," *Conservative Chronicle*, August 28, 2002, p. 23; "Social Security," *Woodland Hills Republican Women Newsletter*, April, 2004; Don Feder, "On Social Security, Dems Lie and Cheat," *Conservative Chronicle*, June 19, 2002, p. 13; David John, senior policy analyst, the Heritage Foundation, "Down Social Security Path," *The Ventura County Star*, Sept. 2, 2001, B-11; David Lambro, "Bush Plans Social Security Revolution," *Conservative Chronicle*, May 16, 2001, p. 3; "Privatizing Social Security: Beyond the Theory," *Cato Policy Report*, May/June, 2001, pp. 6-7; Donald Lambro, "We Can Do Better than Social Security," *Conservative Chronicle*, May 22, 2002, p. 15; Donald Lambro, "Support Widens for Social Security Reform," *Conservative Chronicle*, August 22, 2001, p. 13; Donald Lambro, "Dems Playing Games with Social Security," *Conservative Chronicle*, May 15, 2002, p. 4; Jose Pinera, "Empowering Workers: The Privatization of Social Security in Chile," *Cato's Letter #10*, Cato Institute, 1996; "Other Comments," *Forbes*, March 10, 1997, p. 32; Francisco Margozzini, CEO of the Pension Funds Association, InternationalReports.net, *The Washington Times* 1994-2002, The Cato Institute, Washington, DC; www.csss.gov, President's Commission to Strengthen Social Security.

CHAPTER TWELVE

Sources: President George W. Bush, in Kenneth Walsh, "Command Presence," *US News and World Report*, March 31, 2003, pp. 30-32; President Ronald Reagan, in David Limbaugh, "Calling Terrorists Evil Has Precedent," *Conservative Chronicle*, March 6, 2002, p. 9; General Norman Schwarzkopf, in Rush Limbaugh, *See I Told You So*, Pocket Books, 1993, p. 260; George Washington, First Address to Congress, in Rush Limbaugh, *The Limbaugh Letter*, January, 1997, p. 9; Steven Spielberg, in Chuck Thompson, "Army Buddies," *American Way,* September 1, 2001, pp. 42-52; Winston Churchill, "Now Win the Peace," *The Sunday Telegraph*, opinion.telegraph,co.uk, Spring, 2003, p. 22; Michael Barone, "Waging Postindustrial War," *US World News & Report*, January 20, 2003, p. 25; George Bush, February 1991, *LA Times;* Cap Wienberger, quoted by Hugh Hewitt, KRLA, 2-21-02; Thomas Friedman, *NY Times*; memri.org, *NY Times*; John Leo, "The Truth about

Casualties," *US News and World Report*, March 31, 2003, p. 3; John Anderson, "Iraq's Oil Isn't the Reason for the War," *The Ventura County Star*, March 17, 2003; Abraham Lincoln, *Gettysburg Address*, Nov. 19, 1863, in Rush Limbaugh, *The Limbaugh Letter*, January, 1997, p. 10.

CHAPTER THIRTEEN

Sources: President George W. Bush, in a speech February 11, 2002 at the Medical College of Wisconsin, in Cal Thomas, "Bush Proposes Practical Health Care Reform," Tribune Media Services, *Conservative Chronicle*, February 27, 2002, p. 6; Ted Halstead, "To Guarantee Universal Coverage, Require It," *NY Times*, January 31, 2003, A-27; George Ross Fisher, MD, Internist practicing in Philadelphia and author of *The Hospital that Ate Chicago*, in *USA Today*, "Why Not Try These Health-reform Ideas?" September 27, 1993, A-13; John Breaux, Democratic Senator from Louisiana, "Curing Health Care," *Wall Street Journal*, January 23, 2003, A-14; Thomas Sowell, "Free-Lunch Medicine: Part I," Creators Syndicate, *Conservative Chronicle*, November 26, 2003, p. 6; "Web Sites to Show Drug Rates," *Daily News*, April 12, 2004, N-6; George W. Bush, "It's Déjà Vu All over Again," *President's Message*, Spring, 2003, www.pacificresearch.org, p. 3; Thomas Sowell, "Free-Lunch Medicine: Part III," Creators Syndicate, *Conservative Chronicle*, November 26, 2003, p. 16; Thomas Sowell, "Free-Lunch Medicine: Part I," Creators Syndicate, *Conservative Chronicle*, November 26, 2003, p. 6; Charles Schultz, *Laughing Matters*, Vol. 9-No. 4, p. 140; Patricia Barry, "Why Drugs Costs Less up North," *AARP Bulletin*, June, 2003, pp. 8-10; Thomas Sowell, "Letters about Medical Care," Creators Syndicate, *Conservative Chronicle*, November 26, 2003, p. 21; Julie Appleby, "Health Savings Accounts Get Boost," *USA Today*, March 31, 2004, B-2; Doug Bandow, "Demagogues Will Ruin American Health Care," *Conservative Chronicle*, January 8, 2003, p. 2; Pat Regnier, "He&lth" *Money*, Fall, 2003, pp. 15-19; Ellen McGirt, "How to Get the Right Insurance," *Money*, Fall, 2003, pp. 88-93; Roger Harris, "Low Income Californians Turn to Web for Health," *The Ventura County Star*, December 15, 2003, D-1; Christopher Caggiano, "Taming the Health-Care Monster," *The Whole New Business Catalog*, August, 2003, pp. 98-99; Patricia Barry, "Brands vs. Generics," *AARP Bulletin*, April, 2002, pp. 6-7; Steve Lopez, "Pulling the Plug on This Chronically Sickening Health-care System," *LA Times*, October 19, 2003, B-1; John Walker, CEO of Patient Safety Institute, Plano, TX, "Clinical Information Connectivity Nationwide," *Healthcare Informatics*, October, 2003, pp. 62-63; Mark Hagland, "Reduced Errors Ahead," *Healthcare Informatics*, August, 2003, pp. 31-40; "Short Term Malpractice Fixes Push Partial Cure," *USA Today*, February 11, 2003, A-12; Peter Carbonara, "Diagnosis: Premium Shock RX: Strike," *Money*, May 2003, pp. 115-119; Phyllis Schafly, "Dealing with the High Costs of Health Care," Copley News Service, *Conservative Chronicle*, August 21, 2002, p. 5.

CHAPTER FOURTEEN

Sources: Tony Garza, Ambassador to Mexico, in Samuel Francis, "Republicans Can't Win Amnesty Race," Creators Syndicate, *Conservative Chronicle*, December 11, 2002, p. 19; Linda Bowles, "Ethnic Diversity Is a Double-edged Sword," Creators Syndicate, *Conservative Chronicle*, December 26, 2001, p. 2; Congresswoman Barbara Jordan, in Don Feder, "GOP Balks at Bush's Amnesty Plan," Creators Syndicate, *Conservative Chronicle*, March 27, 2002, p. 3; George W. Bush, in Viet Dinh, "Immigration and American Citizenship," The Proposition, Claremont Institute, June, 2003, p. 1; Abraham Lincoln, July 10, 1858, *The Proposition*, Claremont Institute, June, 2003, p. 1; Victor Davis Hanson, author of *Mexifornia*, in Samuel Francis, "Even Academics Are Seeing the Truth," Creators Syndicate, *Conservative Chronicle*, July 2, 2003, p. 28; Michelle Bustamante, "Bustamante, MEChA and the Media," Creators Syndicate, *Conservative Chronicle*, August 27, 2003, p. 16; Linda Chavez, "Immigration Steals Center Stage in California," Creators Syndicate, *Conservative Chronicle*, August 17, 2003, p. 17; Phyllis Schafly, "Illegal Aliens Raise Cost of our Health Care," Copley News Service , *Conservative Chronicle*, February 5, 2003, p. 29; Rich Lowry, "Why Arnold Should Fight on Immigration" *Conservative Chronicle*, August 27, 2003, p. 7; Rich Lowry, "Liberals Forsaking Americans," *Daily News*, September 1, 2003, N-17; William Buckley, "Why Can't the INS Enforce the Law?" Universal Press Syndicate, *Conservative Chronicle*, November 12, 2003, p. 20; Rachel Swarns, "In Federal Partnership, States and Cities Enforce Immigration Laws," *Ventura County Star,* April 12, 2004, A-1, 6; Thomas Sowell, "Legalizing the Illegals," Creators Syndicate, *Conservative Chronicle*, November 5, 2003, p. 4; Judy Keen and Jim Drinkard, "Debate Erupts on Foreign Workers," *USA Today*, January 8, 2004, A-1; Janet Hook, "Plan Packs Political Bonuses for President," *LA Times,* January 8, 2004, A-1, 15; Donald Lambro, "You CAFTA Like This Deal," United Feature Syndicate, *Conservative Chronicle*, December 31, 2003, p. 9; Christopher Marquis, "Latin America Is Speaking Up," *NY Times*, January 9, 2004, A-1, 6; Mike Smith Cartoon, *USA Today*, January 8, 2004, A-12; George W. Bush, press conference after Saddam's capture, December 15, 2003; William Orme, "Democracy's Success Tied to Economics," *LA Times*, July 24, 2002, A-3; Pat Buchanan, "US Government Refuses to Defend our Borders," Creators Syndicate, *Conservative Chronicle*, November 13, 2002, p. 19; Phyllis Schafly, "US Social Security for Mexicans?" Copley News Service, *Conservative Chronicle*, January 22, 2003, p. 3; Ricardo Alonso-Zaldivar, "Bush Would Open US to Guest Workers," *LA Times,* January 8, 2004, A-1, 14.

CHAPTER FIFTEEN

Sources: Deb Riechmann, "Foreign Worker Program Weighed," *The Ventura County Star*, January 7, 2003, p. A-1, 7; Rich Lowry, "Liberals Forsaking

Americans," *Daily News*, September 1, 2003, N-17; Jennifer Loven, "Bush Proposes New Rights for Illegal Workers," AP, *AOL Online*, 1-7-04; David Abraham, "American Jobs but Not the American Dream," *NY Times*, January 9, 2004, A-21; "Immigration Proposals at a Glance," AP, *AOL Online*, January 6, 2004; Warren Vieth, "Economists See Benefits to Bush Plan," *LA Times*, January 8, 2004, A-14; Deborah Sharp, Paul Davidson, and Tom Kenworthy, "Employers Praise Bush Guest Worker Plan," *USA Today*, January 8, 2004, A-3; Ricardo Alonso-Zaldivar, "Green-card Path Filled with Hurdles," *LA Times*, January 9, 2004, A-9; David Limbaugh, "The Politics of Illegal Immigration," Creators Syndicate, *Conservative Chronicle*, October 23, 2002, p. 15; Mortimer Zuckerman, "Our Rainbow Underclass," *US News and World Report*, September 23, 2002, p. 118; Viet Dinh, "Immigration and American Citizenship," *The Proposition, Claremont Institute*, June, 2003, p. 1; Phyllis Schafly, "Amnesty Puts Profound Questions on Table," *Conservative Chronicle*, August 29, 2001, p. 17; Phyllis Schafly, "Is It Assimilation or an Invasion?" *Conservative Chronicle*, December 5, 2001, p. 5; Tim Weiner, "Of Gringos and Old Grudges: This land Is Their land," *NY Times*, January 9, 2004, A-4; Justin Pritchard, Associated Press, *The Ventura County Star*, December 24, 2003, A-4; Stephen Frank, *California Political News and Views*, January 5, 2004, stephenfrank@sbcglobal.net; Louis Uchitelle, "Plan May Lure More to Enter US Illegally, Experts Say," *NY Times*, January 9, 2004, A-10; Arizona Congressman Hayworth, on Laura Ingraham, *The Laura Ingraham Show*, http://www.krla870.com; Donna Leinwand, "National ID in Development," *USA Today*, January 22, 2002, A-2; Martha Irvine, "Scanners Now Spot Fake IDs," *The Ventura County Star*, October 13, 2003, A-3; Elton Gallegly, "Price Too High to Accept IDs," *The Ventura County Star*, March 23, 2003, B-12; David Collins, "Fox Should Worry about His Country," *The Ventura County Star*, December 24, 2003, B-9; Justin Prichard, "Raid Focus Shifts," *Daily News*, December 1, 2003, p. 5; Samuel Francis, "The Heat Is on for Amnesty," Creators Syndicate, *Conservative Chronicle*, November 5, 2003, p. 5; Michelle Malkin, "Close Birthright Citizenship Loopholes," *Conservative Chronicle*, July 16, 2003, p. 16; Samuel Francis, "It's a Stretch to Claim Hispanic Vote Is in Play," Creators Syndicate, *Conservative Chronicle*, November 5, 2003, p. 6.

EPILOGUE

Sources: Will Rogers, in Paula McSpadden Love, *The Will Rogers Book*, in *Forbes*, November 7, 1994, p. 28; Winston Churchill, in Charles Henning, ed. *The Wit and Wisdom of Politics*, Fulcrum Inc., Golden, CO, 1989, p. 81; Robert C. Byrd, *The Great American Bathroom Book II*, Compact Classics, Salt Lake City, UT, 1993, pp. 525-535.

THE DINNER